Rubber Stamping

Published in 2016 by
Laurence King Publishing Ltd
361–373 City Road
London EC1V 1LR
United Kingdom
T +44 (0)20 7841 6900
F +44 (0)20 7841 6910
enquiries@laurenceking.com
www.laurenceking.com

ISBN
978-178-0678-658

Design
John Dowling/Mucho

Printed in China

Rubber Stamping

Get creative with stamps, rollers and other printmaking techniques

Stephen Fowler
Foreword by Rob Ryan

Laurence King
Publishing

Contents

Foreword
Rob Ryan

Rob Ryan
Fairytale character,
multiple stamp, 2012

When I was a child I quickly learned that the mark of the rubber stamp was the mark of authority. Our textbooks held the name of the school firmly rubber stamped in navy blue on the inside pages. 'Do not deface or steal' was the accompanying message. It was the brand of ownership. At the public library, after choosing the books I wished to take out, I presented them in a neat pile to the lady at the desk where she stamped each one with a date, which really meant, 'Bring this back by then or you're in big trouble'. Stamps had meanings. Also, if there were lots of date stamps inside, it meant the book was popular and thus a good one; if only a few, it meant it was unpopular and thus boring. All of this information just from some stamps!

My mother was a shorthand typist. On rare visits to her office I had the chance to rubber stamp myself. The satisfaction of reading the actual stamp back to front and then pressing it down on to paper to see it printed the right way around was immense. I felt the power of stamping run through my veins for the first time. Some of the words on the stamps – 'Received', 'Urgent' or 'Approved' – I understood even though they seemed hardly exciting; other words – 'Pending', 'Audit', 'Void' and 'Credited' – seemed mysterious, belonging to an elusive adult world of boredom that was thankfully still beyond my reach. They remained meaningless as I magically made patterns from their shapes.

As the years passed, I realized that the wielders of the stamps held the reins of power. Your destiny lay in their hands: whether 'PASS' or 'FAIL' was stamped upon your file could define your future. 'Accept' or 'Reject' upon a visa would change a life forever. What could be sweeter, then, than to take this weapon of officialdom and turn it into something that wields beauty rather than power? The stamp of approval would become meaningless in an artist's hands because art neither craves nor requires approval for its actions; it is, thankfully beyond both of these things.

So little is needed to begin to make so much. Some rubber, a knife, an inkpad – that is all. Not even paper is required: use your own body as a canvas if you wish, for this art form is printmaking at its simplest and purest.

The self-reliance of rubber stamping is liberating, since you absolutely own the entire means of production. You don't have to answer to anyone and are now free to set off with just a few simple stamps on a journey that could take you anywhere. The joy of repetition is now at your fingertips and you can begin to build up bigger and bigger images, stamp by stamp, as a builder can build an entire house from one size of brick.

Within the pages of this inspiring book by Stephen Fowler are countless ideas and suggestions to guide you on your rubber-stamping journey. Now it is your turn to make your stamp upon the world, a chance to make it a less authoritative, but more beautiful and exciting place for everyone. So I guess you'd better get started.

Introduction

I was introduced to rubber stamping as an undergraduate by the printmaker, Steve Hoskins. He brought a bag of WHSmith erasers to a workshop he was giving and taught a small group of us art students and tutors to carve our own stamps from them. I still have the limited edition rubber-stamped publication we made together on that day almost 25 years ago.

The democratic and collaborative aspect of that day reminds me of art movements such as Fluxus. In fact, some of my art tutors at Harrow Art College had been involved with this international movement during the 1960s and '70s, when they themselves were students. And rubber stamping – most notably in the innovative work of Ray Johnson – played an important role in the postal correspondence of the Fluxus network, with its aim of circumventing the gallery system.

Andy Warhol and Julia Warhola
The Wonderful World of Fleming-Joffe, cover drawing, c. 1961

These were not the first artists to experiment with the medium, however. As early as 1912, Aleksei Kruchenykh, a Russian Futurist poet, featured rubber stamps in his artist books. Around the same time, Marcel Duchamp devised a rubber-stamp chess set so he could print each move and play by correspondence and, in 1919, Kurt Schwitters started to make his 'stamp drawings' from official rubber stamps.

Instances of pure inventiveness abound throughout the history of rubber stamping. For the most part these occurred out of necessity and often during periods of oppression such as war, or political and judicial clampdowns. In 1912, to bypass a Parisian law banning the distribution of advertising paper bills on the city streets, a hawker made his shoe soles into rubber stamps and, in doing so, littered the pavements with ink impressions instead. In far more dangerous conditions, during World War II, prisoners of war also used shoe soles, wellington boots and even soap to carve fake authorization stamps with the aid of a razor blade to forge paperwork and passports. In Eastern European countries during the Cold War, when the mere possession of a rubber stamp was sometimes unlawful, artists such as Pawel Petasz and Henry Bzdok carved rubber stamps from erasers.

Romanian-American illustrator Saul Steinberg explored and questioned the power of officialdom through the intentionally unreadable stamps and seals he produced during the 1960s. According to his biographer, Deirdre Bai, he amassed over four hundred rubber stamps to be used in his illustrations: 'men on horseback, soldiers on foot, and other figures on animals in various poses and activities … but he insisted that he needed only a core group of fifty "to render space nature, technology".' Meanwhile, Steinberg's contemporary, Andy Warhol, included patterns and symbols made from hand-carved rubber stamps in his early illustrations (facing page), and artist and educator Sister Corita Kent taught her students how to make rubber stamps from erasers – her famous set of rules for Los Angeles Immaculate Heart College (below) is in fact composed from carved rubber stamps.

David Mekelburg
Immaculate Heart College Art Department Rules, c. 1968

IMMACULATE HEART COLLEGE ART DEPARTMENT RULES

Rule 1 FIND A PLACE YOU TRUST AND THEN TRY TRUSTING IT FOR A WHILE.

Rule 2 GENERAL DUTIES OF A STUDENT: PULL EVERYTHING OUT OF YOUR TEACHER; PULL EVERYTHING OUT OF YOUR FELLOW STUDENTS.

Rule 3 GENERAL DUTIES OF A TEACHER: PULL EVERYTHING OUT OF YOUR STUDENTS.

Rule 4 CONSIDER EVERYTHING AN EXPERIMENT.

Rule 5 BE SELF DISCIPLINED. THIS MEANS FINDING SOMEONE WISE OR SMART AND CHOOSING TO FOLLOW THEM. TO BE DISCIPLINED IS TO FOLLOW IN A GOOD WAY. TO BE SELF DISCIPLINED IS TO FOLLOW IN A BETTER WAY.

Rule 6 NOTHING IS A MISTAKE. THERE'S NO WIN AND NO FAIL. THERE'S ONLY MAKE.

Rule 7 The only rule is work. IF YOU WORK IT WILL LEAD TO SOMETHING. IT'S THE PEOPLE WHO DO ALL OF THE WORK ALL THE TIME WHO EVENTUALLY CATCH ON TO THINGS.

Rule 8 DON'T TRY TO CREATE AND ANALYSE AT THE SAME TIME. THEY'RE DIFFERENT PROCESSES.

Rule 9 BE HAPPY WHENEVER YOU CAN MANAGE IT. ENJOY YOURSELF. IT'S LIGHTER THAN YOU THINK.

Rule 10 "WE'RE BREAKING ALL OF THE RULES. EVEN OUR OWN RULES. AND HOW DO WE DO THAT? BY LEAVING PLENTY OF ROOM FOR X QUANTITIES." JOHN CAGE

HELPFUL HINTS: ALWAYS BE AROUND. COME OR GO TO EVERYTHING. ALWAYS GO TO CLASSES. READ ANYTHING YOU CAN GET YOUR HANDS ON. LOOK AT MOVIES CAREFULLY, OFTEN. SAVE EVERYTHING-IT MIGHT COME IN HANDY LATER. THERE SHOULD BE NEW RULES NEXT WEEK.

To this day, artists and illustrators keep returning to rubber stamps as a form of graphic expression. Natsuko Oshima, a Tokyo-based illustrator uses the inhabitants of her city as inspiration for her rubber-stamped zines: Tokyo Salaryman Stamp and Tokyoite Stamp, both feature beautifully observed figures of city folk performing simple public rituals, such as buying raisins or shoveling snow (facing page). Artist Jeremy Deller, on the other hand, used rubber stamps as an interactive element in his 2013 Venice Biennale British Pavilion show (below). Everyone could stamp and take home a printed souvenir of two of the murals featured prominently in the exhibition.

This idea of inclusivity is at the heart of the creative democracy of rubber stamping and is something I too have tried to reflect in the pages of this book. While most of the prints featured are my own, many are by other rubber stampers who I find inspiring or with whom I have had the opportunity to stamp collaboratively.

EQUIPMENT AND TECHNICAL APPROACHES

This first chapter presents the bare bones of rubber stamping. All you'll need to start is an eraser, pencil, scalpel, ink pad and something to print on. You'll no doubt be tempted to leap straight in to the projects included later, but working through the instructions given in the next few pages first will set you up with some handy techniques. You may also find it helpful to revisit this chapter if you are, say, looking for technical assistance in the finer details of multicoloured stamping, or struggling to position a stamp perfectly.

Materials, tools and equipment

It's important to have a well-stocked and organized equipment box or studio. An entire day can be wasted purchasing missing knives or stamp pads, for instance. What follows is a list of the essential equipment and materials used in the making of rubber stamps and other alternative printmaking methods, such as roller printing. For specific items required for each project, please refer to the project materials list on the relevant page. Specialist suppliers are outlined at the back of the book, along with useful books and websites.

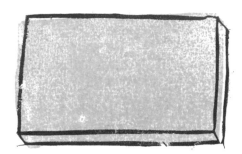

Purpose-made rubber-stamp carving blocks

Once you have exhausted the possibilities of carved erasers, advance to Speedball Speedy-Carve block for this dependable soft pink material is excellent and the best large scale carving block on the market. Its cushion-like softness makes for satisfying impressions. Unlike some cheap erasers, it won't dry and crumble, so all of your hard work won't go to waste!

Other blocks I use include 'soft-cut' lino, designed as an easier carving lino. It can be employed as stamp material and is also available in circular discs. It is dense so a soft cushion material such as neoprene craft foam needs to be placed under the paper when you come to print. Funky Foam is the leading brand, available in sizes A5, A4 and A3. Pound-shop versions work just as well but only come in an A5 size. Sheets can be cut into all manner of shapes and be indented with pens and pencils. Mount the foam on pieces of wood, for a firmer grip.

Soft-Kut is a very thick rubbery sheet and, again, very good material for large rubber stamps. It's durable and has a good 'cushion' for printing. However it's rather difficult to obtain outside the United States.

Pencils and pens

Use soft 2B pencils for drawing and transferring rubber-stamp designs. Biros transfer graphite brilliantly and are great for repeating a drawing transfer if needs be.

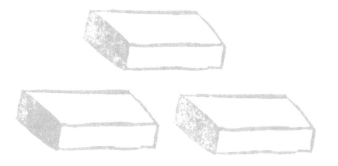

Erasers

I would advise picking up the plasticized vinyl variety of eraser as these are firm, easy to carve and don't crumble after frequent use. Avoid brands that have embossed logos, as these will interfere with your stamp relief. Inked logos can be easily removed by placing parcel tape on the logo and removing the tape: the sticky-backed tape will remove the ink. Buy erasers in bulk from pound shops and websites, where bargains are to be found. Look out for novelty-shaped and -sized rubbers in tourist and museum gift shops.

Knives

I would be lost without my Swann-Morton scalpel – I use the 3 handle and 10a blades. It is an essential piece of equipment for any rubber stamper. It's excellent for carving eraser stamps, pipe lagging and scaffolding foam. Keep a large stock of blades. I also use extendable craft knives; these are excellent for cutting paper and card, and for cropping zines and artists books. I keep a Stanley knife at hand for all those heavy-duty cutting jobs, such as cutting greyboard. With all knives and carving tools it's important that they are sharpened or that blades are replaced when blunt.

Stamp pads

Generic stamp pads found in stationery shops, used for officialdom office stamping, come in very vivid, strong bright colours. Unfortunately if exposed to daylight for too long they will eventually fade and the pads quickly dry out after frequent use, (so top them up with stamp ink from a bottle).

In contrast, craft and artist stamp pads never seem to dry up. Water-based dye, pigment and oil based pads are all available. It's worth experimenting to see which is most suitable and effective for specific projects and tasks, water-based pads are ideal for overprinting; oil-based pigment dye are opaque, print on wood and produce the best detailed impressions, while pigment pads are renowned for their fluorescent inks. Each brand of stamp pad has their own particular set of colours – test them all and collect your favourite ones. The majority of stamp pads have raised pads. This allows them to be used with all types of stamps including the oversized. Specialist UV light stamp pads and food stamp pads are also available.

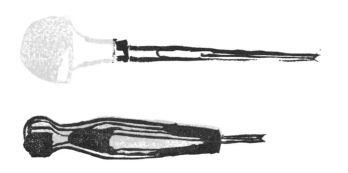

Relief-printing gouges

A scalpel will suffice for most of your carving but it's handy to have a small range of relief-printing gouges at your disposal. I recommend buying a simple box of lino/wood-cutting tools, either the Speedball brand of grip handles with its assortment of five changeable cutters or a box of pencil-type cutters. Either one will effortlessly remove large areas of rubber or eraser material. For tricky detailed carving jobs, use either Swiss or Japanese extra-fine cutting tools, available in U and V shaped varieties.

Simple relief-printing equipment and relief-printing rollers

Mix your relief printing inks to the desired colours or required consistency on ink block – a piece of tempered glass, Perspex, or Formica, for example – using a plastic or metal spatula. I recommend buying an inexpensive economy roller such as the Speedball Deluxe roller for 'inking up'; they have a firm and yet soft quality ideal for clay printing, found-object stamping and even plaster block stamping.

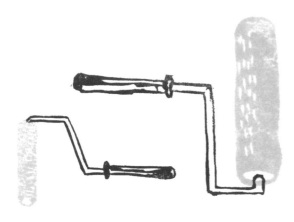

Paint rollers

Small and large paint rollers will fit most foam tubes, but it is worth checking size compatibility before making any purchases. I find large rollers from pound shops are the right size for scaffolding foam, and small radiator rollers are ideally suited to pipe lagging.

Cleaning equipment

To avoid polluting a stamp pad with different ink it is essential to clean your rubber stamps between colour changes, employing either watered-down window-cleaner (1 part cleaner to 3 parts water) or water with a spot of washing-up liquid. Use a spray to dispense the solution, and then, with a paper towel, soak up the liquid and leave to dry. Don't rub the stamp as this will wear it down. An ink stain will remain, but won't affect future printing.

Vegetable oil will remove oil-based inks; remember to degrease the stamp afterwards with your liquid spray solution. Oil will also remove any graphite mistakes made while transferring pencil designs to erasers.

A sink of warm soapy water will wash away water-based inks from tools used in adapted-roller printing. For a deeper clean, use a household paint brush or an old toothbrush. Allow your tools to dry before they are used again.

Adapted roller

To adapt a paint roller, use either scaffolding protection foam, foam tube swimming aids or pipe lagging such as Mangers (Water Regulation Bylaw 49 pipe insulation), depending on the size of roller you have. These firm and dense tubes are easy to carve and create excellent results.

Glue

PVA glue is a brilliant all-rounder; it's surprisingly strong and quick drying. Use it to permanently adhere wood and greyboard mounts to rubber stamps, and in the making of found-object stamps, for example. I highly recommend 'strong' PVA.

I have found UHU to be the best glue for repairing carved foam used in the making of adapted rollers and for sealing the pre-slit brands of pipe lagging.

Paper

Use either photocopy paper or tracing-paper for drawing and transferring graphite-pencil designs onto erasers or rubber-stamp sheets (tracing-paper is excellent for lining up eraser and design, and can be used to trace drawings and pictures from sketchbooks).

A rubber-stamp print impression can bleed. To prevent this, use a paper which is part wood pulp and part cotton, such as Canaletto hot-pressed paper or Zerkall (both approximately 145 gsm). This cotton- mix will absorb the ink. Using this same paper for roller printing books will help avoid any paper curling (due to layers of thick ink) and ensure that the stock is light enough for folding into pamphlet books. Wallpaper lining is great for all other roller-printing projects: it's cheap and absorbent, to boot.

Redeem (130 gsm) recycled paper is great for creative rubbings. The off-white colour complements a black rubbing stick. Arboreta cream or white cartridge paper is an excellent general printing paper suitable for many of the excercises in this book.

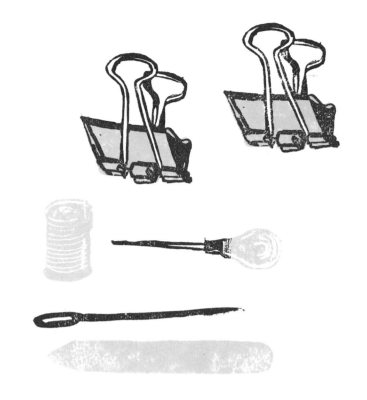

Bookbinding materials

A simple bookbinding kit consists of a bone folder to fold paper, an awl to create holes of stitching and binding clips to hold pages in place when binding with a needle and linen thread. Alternatives to linen thread include red and white butcher's twine, button thread or even dental floss.

Tape

Parcel tape is handy for removing printed logos on erasers. Simply place a length of the tape on the logo and peel off, and after a few goes the logo will disappear.

Invisible tape, such as Scotch Magic tape, is useful for holding a paper in place when transferring graphite design onto erasers or for adhering paper when carving designs into foam tubes. Masking tape is also essential.

Relief-printing ink

Depending on the project, there are a variety of specialist inks you can choose from. In adapted-roller printing, for instance, a lot of ink will be required; I recommend cheap water-based ink, such as Ocaldo or Seawhite block-printing ink. These inks, however, take some time to dry so, for a faster-drying version, use Schmincke lino ink.

For found-object stamps and plaster printing use Caligo relief printing ink. Just like any good oil-based ink, it leaves a rich and satisfying stamp impression and, as it is water-based, tools and blocks are easily cleaned.

How to carve a rubber stamp

The first step – and the most essential – is learning to carve your first stamp. Keep your design as simple as possible at this stage so that you can focus on mastering the technique; don't trip yourself up with anything overly complicated. A scalpel is excellent for carving tiny detail. It makes the same V-shaped gouge as a lino-cutting tool, but in two movements – first the left and then the right side of the 'V'. Some people find carving with a scalpel is an easy transition to make; others (like myself) take a little longer to master it. But don't give up – after a few goes it will just click!

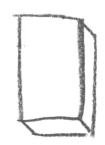

Step 1. Take your eraser and draw around it on paper.

Step 2. Using a pencil, draw a picture in the box.

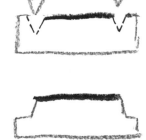

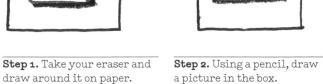

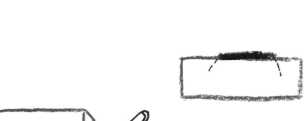

Step 7. Cut away the white areas, holding the scalpel at a 45-degree angle.

Step 8. Cut the eraser with a series of V-shaped grooves.

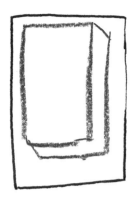

Step 3. Place the eraser back on the picture square.

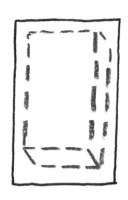

Step 4. Flip it over.

Step 5. Scribble on the back to transfer the picture.

Step 6. The transferred picture.

Step 9. Your picture is now raised in relief and ready to be printed.

Step 10. Gently touch your stamp several times on an ink pad; don't over ink it.

Step 11. To get a good print, apply hard, even pressure.

Step 12. Your finished rubber stamp print.

How to make two-colour prints

At a certain point you will want to make prints featuring more than one colour. The simplest way to achieve a two-colour print is by adding a second colour to an existing print. You can then create further colour separations if you wish by simply repeating the same steps. Try the following exercise for a sense of how multicoloured prints work. You will see, too, that stamping over the top of previous impressions creates additional colours. This is called overprinting, which is covered in more detail on page 60.

Step 1. Print a rubber stamp using a light-coloured ink pad, such as blue or red.

Step 2. With a soft 2B pencil add a second colour. The contrast of pencil and ink will help you envisage your two-colour print.

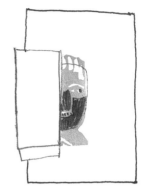

Step 3. Repeat the stamp-carving instructions from pages 18-19, placing a new eraser on top of the print/drawing.

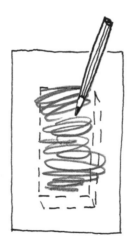

Step 4. Flip the eraser and paper over and scribble on the back of the paper.

Step 5. The second-colour drawing transferred to the eraser.

Step 6. Carve away the white areas of the eraser, leaving the dark pencil drawing in relief.

Step 7. To aid print registration (see overleaf), trim around the stamp, removing large areas of white eraser.

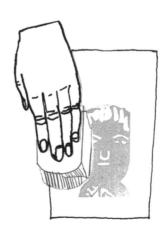

Step 8. Ink up the stamp and print over the first colour.

Step 9. Your final two-colour rubber-stamp print.

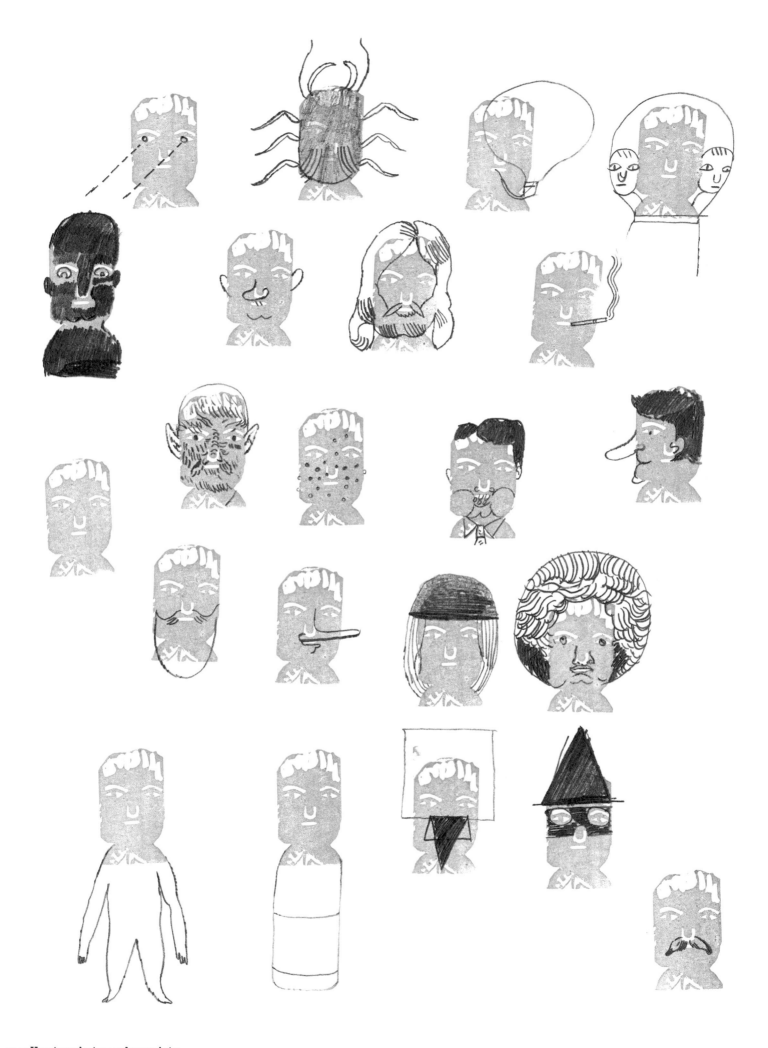

Registering multicoloured prints

You will need:

Rubber stamps

Ink pads

Rubber-stamp positioner (these can be purchased, or made from thick board or wood)

Paper

Tracing-paper (90 gsm)

Printing multicoloured prints by eye creates dynamic results (see pictures on facing page), but if you want a print positioned perfectly – lining up a repeat pattern, or combining two colours to make a third – then working by eye can be a very frustrating activity. This can be solved by using a stamp positioner.

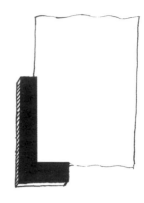

Step 1. This print consists of 4 components: water, jar, string and goldfish. Ink up and print the first rubber stamp (the water) on a piece of paper.

Step 2. Place a small piece of tracing paper in the corner of the rubber-stamp positioner.

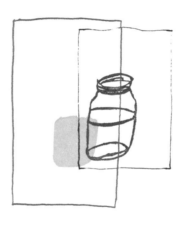

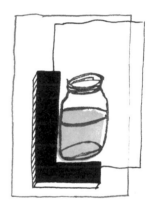

Step 3. Now ink up the second rubber stamp (the jar). Position the stamp so that it sits in the same left-hand corner, then press down and print on the tracing-paper.

Step 4. Line up the first and second colours by placing the tracing-paper over the stamp impression on the paper and moving it to the desired position.

Step 5. Place the positioner against the bottom left-hand corner of the tracing paper.

Step 6. Remove the tracing-paper. Ink up the second rubber stamp and, once again, line it up in the corner of the positioner. Press down.

Step 7. A two-coloured rubber stamp print.

To add the string and goldfishes, repeat Steps 2 to 7 until complete.

Misregistered prints

Misregistered multicoloured prints including these ones of bearded men by Tavan Maneetapho (below) and of dinosaurs by Abigail Mortimer (bottom) are reminiscent of 1960s comics.

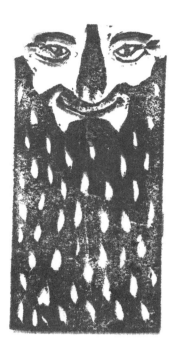

Reduction printing

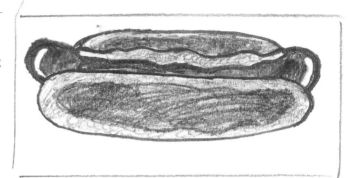

You will need:

Pencil

Eraser

Scalpel and/or relief-printing tools

Ink pads

Rubber-stamp positioner

Paper

This traditional method, whereby a single block is carved in stages between each print impression, can be used to make multicoloured prints from a single eraser. Through a series of carvings, inkings and stampings, an edition of coloured prints will slowly emerge as the eraser is gradually eaten away. When it comes to layering colours, oil-based inks are opaque and will happily print in this way.

Step 1. Draw around the eraser to establish the size of your artwork. Inside this outline make a tonal drawing of the stamp to help you plan the carving stages – the lightest areas are removed first; the darkest areas are left until last.

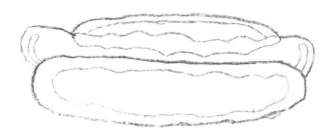

Step 2. Trace a simplified line plan of the tonal areas onto a piece of tracing-paper.

Step 3. Flip the tracing-paper over, place it on the eraser, then scribble over the back to transfer the plan to the eraser.

Step 4. Remove the white areas of the stamp design, following the carving instructions on pages 18–19.

Step 5. Ink up and print the lightest colour, then carve away the areas that need to remain in this colour.

Step 6. Ink up and print the next colour, then, as before, carve away the areas that need to remain in this colour. Use the stamp positioner to line up the colours accurately.

Step 7. Repeat this process until you have your finished print.

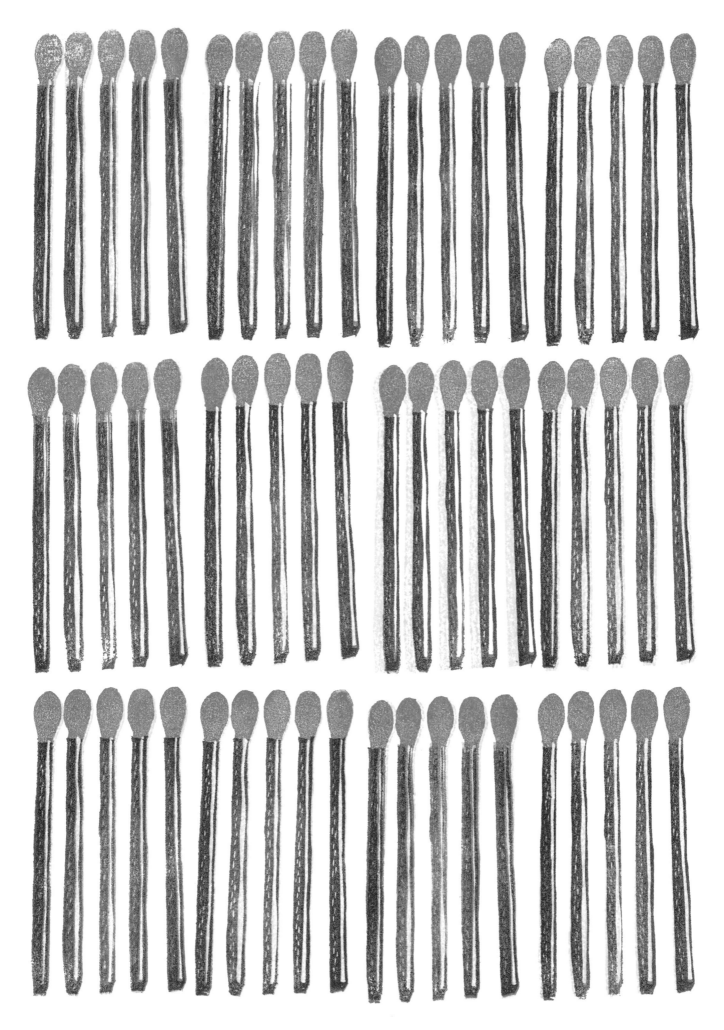

Masking

You will need:

Rubber stamps

Post-it notes

Ink pads

Scalpel

Paper

Masking is a technique that allows you to establish foreground, middle-ground and background picture planes without having to worry about unintentional confusion between overlapping prints. With a bit of imagination you can create the illusion of space, and a strong sense of narrative.

Step 1. Start by printing the tree (foreground) on the paper.

Step 2. Print the same stamp on a Post-it note.

Step 5. Print the twins on another Post-it note, cut them out and mask the original printed twins.

Step 6. Print another tree stamp (background) over the masked areas.

Step 3. Using a scalpel, cut out the tree. (The more accurately cut out, the better the masking results.) Stick the cut-out Post-it note over the original stamp print.

Step 4. The first stamp is now masked, so you can print the (middle-ground) stamp on top – some brightly coloured twins.

Step 7. Print the tree on another Post-it note, cut it out and mask it again. Stamp a third and final tree.

Step 8. Mask the last tree, and then stamp a house to complete the picture. Peel away the Post-its to reveal the print.

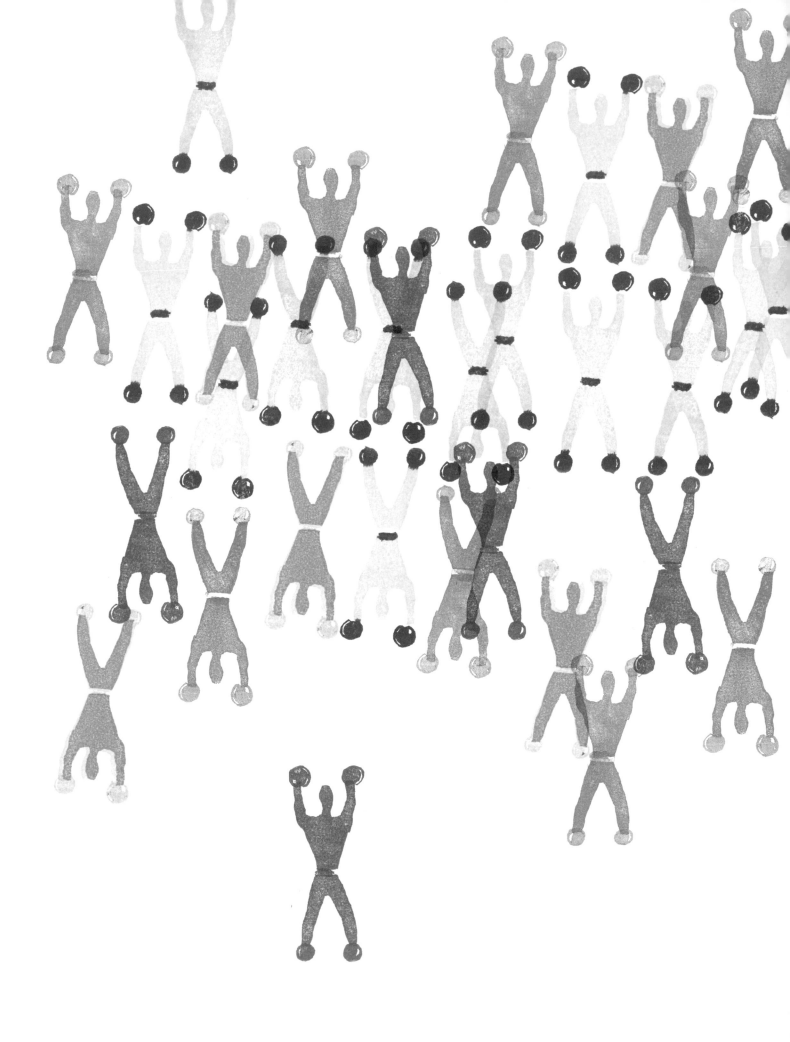

PROJECTS

I never tire of rubber stamping. Even the simplest approaches can lead to something unexpected, and I'm constantly surprised by (and jealous of) what others manage to create. It can be a collaborative process, too – group activities can take a stamp far beyond its creator's initial ideas. In fact, it was working with some students and witnessing their enthusiasm and ideas for stamping that revived my own interest in the subject. Many of the projects in this chapter have also come about as a result of observing and interacting with other practitioners.

The visuals for this chapter have been carefully selected so that you will be able to interpret them at a glance, leaving you ready to create your own original work. Try making your own ink pads, constructing a simple toy, or even try stamping the world – and people – around you. Rubber stamping is such an immediate and intuitive process that the projects here will be the start of all sorts of new directions.

Getting started

Your first decision will be what to carve. I encourage newcomers to focus on something simple, not only as a means of mastering the carving technique, but also to avoid the restrictions of overly complex ideas. It is in the making that ideas are generated, as one step leads to the next. Start by carving a simple positive outline – a living thing or manmade object, a descriptive silhouette or a simplified geometric version, such as these examples by Elisha Marshall, Lorna Scobie and Tim King (right, far right and bottom right). Consider including negative shapes or white lines in your block, too, as these will help create a dynamic, expressive print like the ones produced by John Bentley, Helen Davies and Matt Ferguson and friends (facing page, left, centre and bottom right).

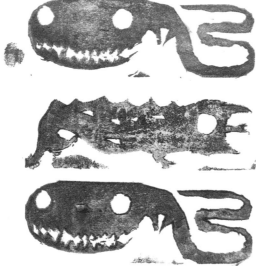

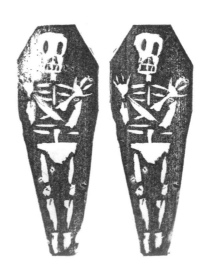

KAVVA

Predictable PIVO

THREE EYES MEN

FIREY MONSIEUR

OUCH

Silhouette stamps

These are stamps of things that I'm either preoccupied with, and/or have associations with rubber, such as spiders, gloves, inner tubes, dinosaurs, seaweed and saints.

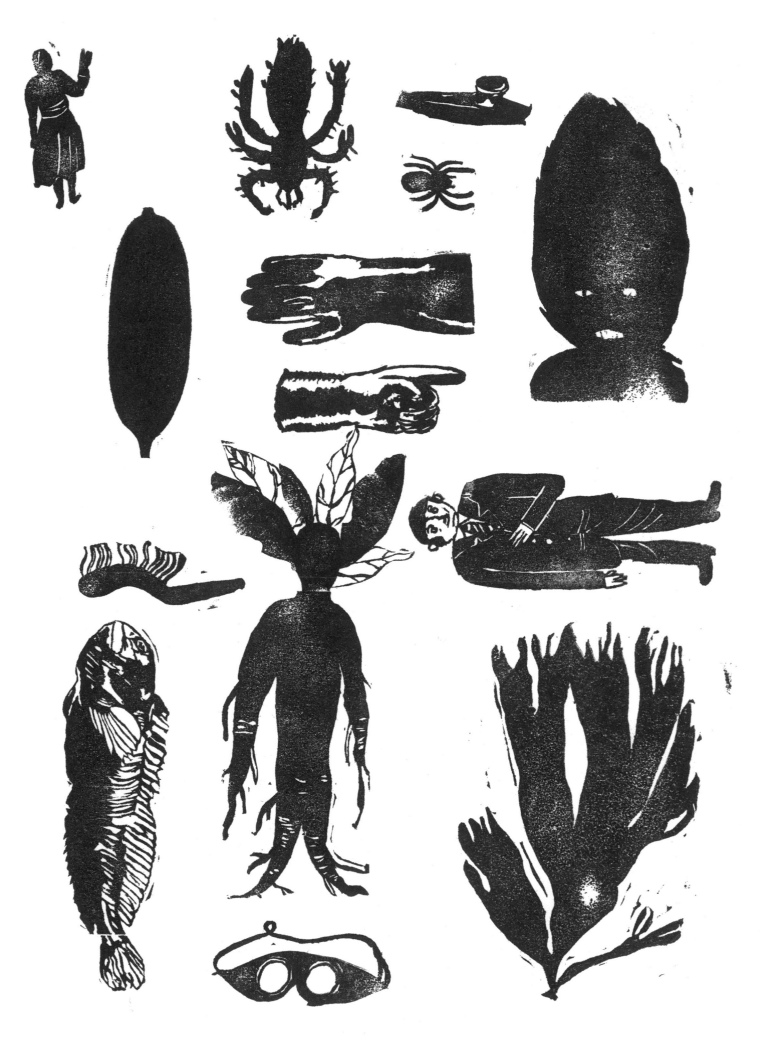

Repeat printing

As soon as you have carved your first rubber stamp you will immediately want to start printing your motif repeatedly across a piece of paper. This is a very natural response, and a satisfying exercise! However, there are a number of methods of repetition that can be used, depending on the motif, and the purpose of the print. I have loosely categorized these as random repeats, continuous repeats, constructions and complicated configurations.

Random repeats

This is when a motif is printed with no preconceived order. It is particularly effective when stamping a visual representation of an object. A spider can grow into a cluster, a fly can become a swarm, or people can congregate to form a crowd. Yan Dan Wong takes this approach even further by merging rubber stamping and reportage illustration – note her use of shadow and how she subtly alters each silhouette (this page).

Continuous repeats

Continuous repeats are ongoing lengths of joined-up motifs. As with random repeats, taking a playful, inventive approach will provide you with loads of picture-making potential. Plants are a natural choice of subject-matter here, for example Ruby Smith's healthy cactus and Rosie Bell Ryott's gnarly tree trunk (both facing page, far right), as are circular patterns such as those by Lily Xue and Jackie Kirk (right and below). Roads, rivers and tracks are excellent themes as well, such as this Scalextric layout (below right), recreated during a workshop at Chesterfield College in Derbyshire.

Constructions

You can also approach repeat printing in a slightly different way, treating your rubber stamps as building blocks – squares, rectangles, arcs, cylinders – and using them to construct buildings. These can be as simple or as complicated as you like, from the simplicity of Brutalism, through to the coloured brick and decorative detail of the Victorian period. Make a list of the simple elements you will need. Carve them and then start using your stamps to build houses, streets and towns without worrying about architectural rules – your buildings will never fall down.

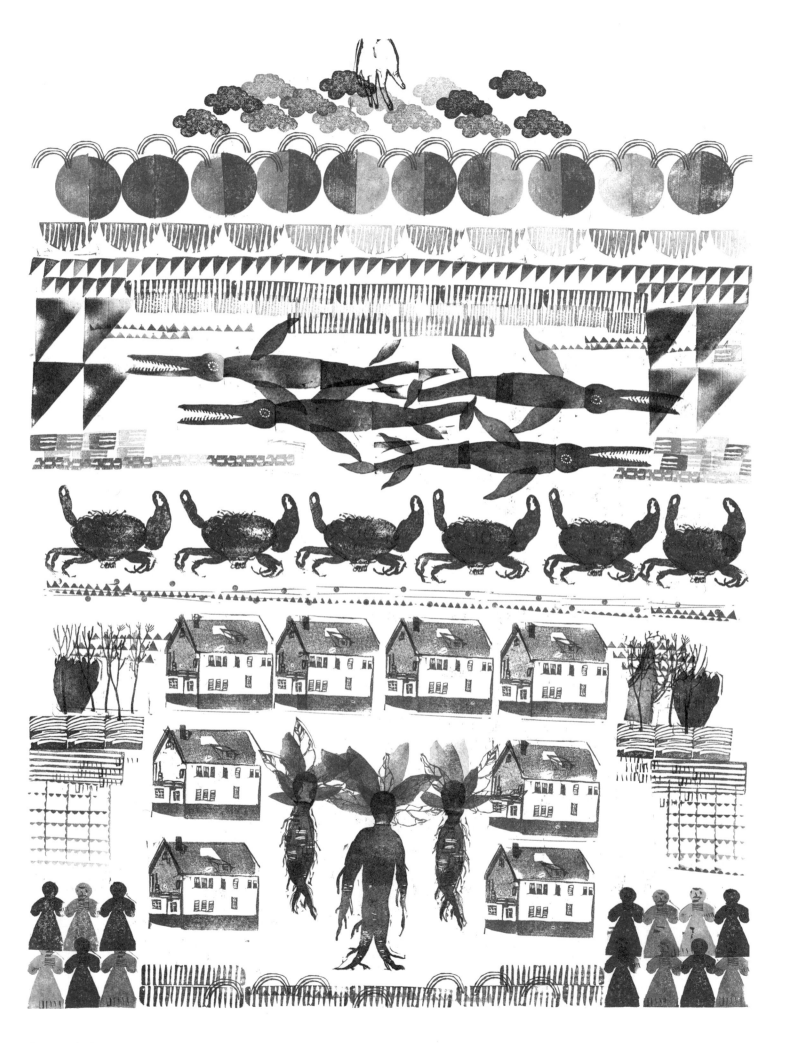

Complicated configurations

I've always approached block repeat patterns with a sense of wonder combined with terror, hence the label 'complicated configurations'! The secret is that they are actually far easier to understand once you have already made them. As with many things, it's through doing that you start to gain confidence. All you need is a way to make a start, so begin by recreating these simple configurations.

Step 1. A single squared notched motif.

Step 2. A 90-degree clockwise rotation repeat.

Step 3. On its head and with an anticlockwise 90-degree rotation.

Step 4. One on top of each other, upwards, sideways and upside down.

Step 5. Side-to-side layered notches.

Step 6. A half-drop repeat.

Step 7. Side to side and back to back.

Step 8. Alternating back to back.

Step 9. Side to side, back to back and tips touching.

Tip: When you have a sense of how these repeat patterns work, follow the diagrams again, this time using some new motifs. Consider introducing a second colour for an extra challenge.

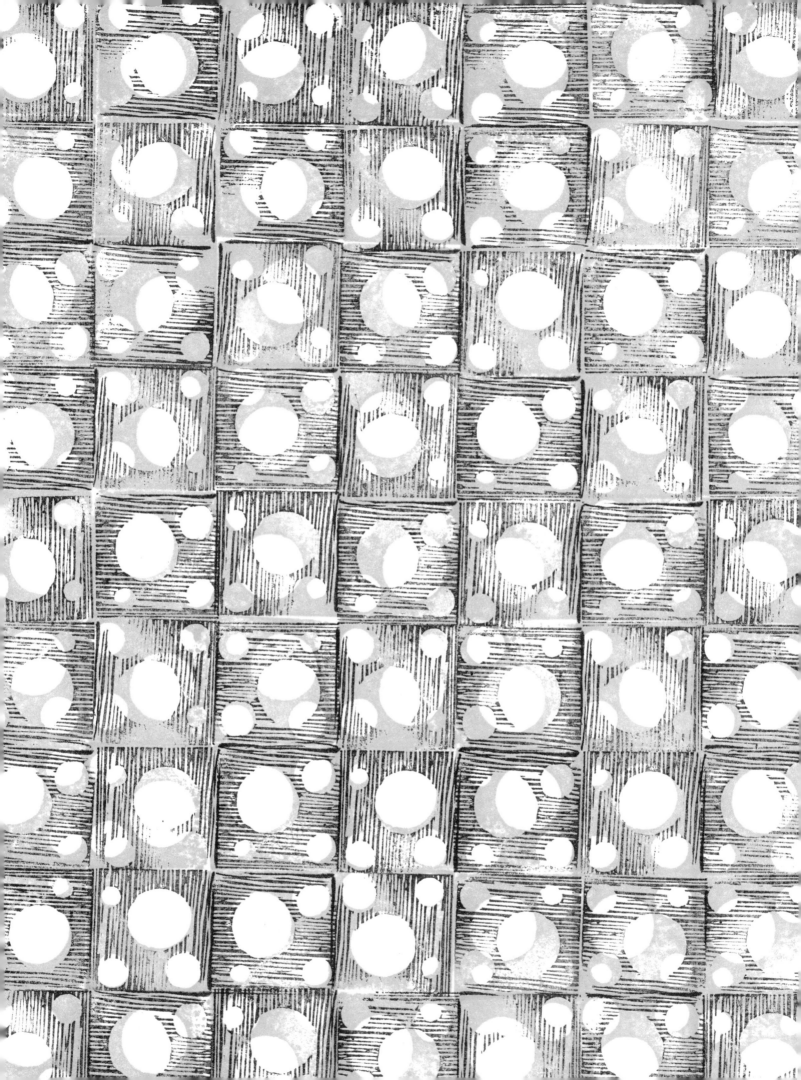

Jantze Tullett (this page) approaches her pattern making without planning ahead too much, naturally creating repeats using simple motif rotations, drop patterns and multicoloured layering. Her free-flowing patterns often break the traditional rules of pattern repeats, creating designs resembling patchwork that change colour and rotation midway, leading to unexpected and exciting outcomes.

Applied patterns

It can really help to have a home for your patterns. The most obvious applications are decorative endpapers, gift wrap and wallpaper, but there are many other possibilities, too. Alexandra Czinczel uses patterns to illustrate three-dimensional objects – see her pop-up ant farm (below). See too how Haley Dixon's button-maze book (right) and my own paper suit (facing page) take the idea a step further, allowing patterns to transcend the sum of their parts to become three-dimensional 'things' in their own right.

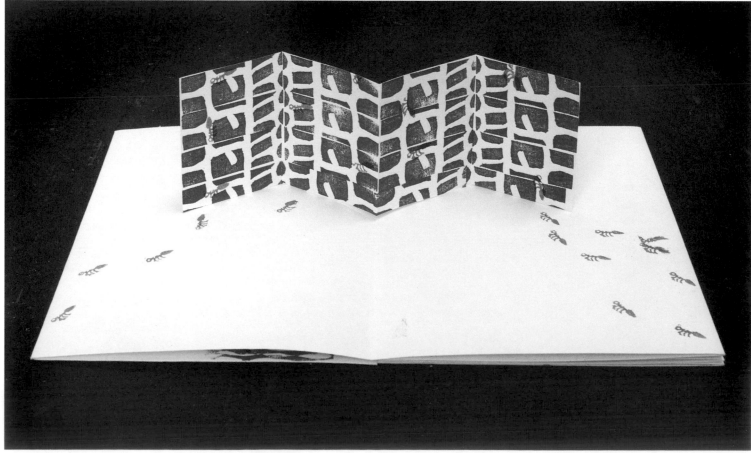

Collaborative printing

Collaborating with other rubber stampers can be more helpful than you think, breaking patterns of thought and making, and helping you to reinterpret and transform your work.

Exquisite corpse

This game of chance, in which each player creates part of a drawing or text without being able to see the previous player's contribution, was invented by the Surrealists. Using this technique to create a figure through an amalgamation of body parts makes a great rubber-stamp activity. Gather a group of friends and instruct each person to make three body sections – head, torso, and legs and feet. (You can extend this to more sections if you wish – hat, hands, etc.) Mix the stamps up, place several sheets of paper on a table and start printing the body parts, each person moving along the table printing randomly. After a few minutes, people tend to loosen up and make choices they wouldn't have dreamt of before.

These corpses (this page), created at University of the West of England's Centre for Fine Print Research, have strayed into the world of mythical creatures and fabulous beasts with their mismatched jumble of body parts.

Working independently, Bjørn Rune Lie (facing page) combines tree trunks, geometric shapes and bearded heads to create his wondrous hybrids.

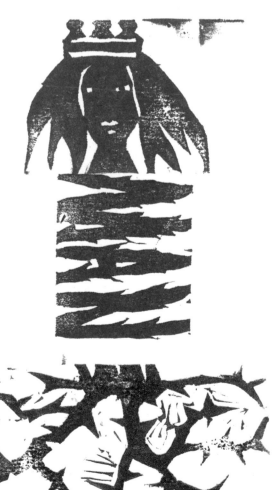

Identikit portraits

You can also use the same technique to produce a portrait, identikit-style. Instead of body parts, each player carves facial features. Having several participants will ensure that each feature is distinctive: hooked noses, beady eyes, shell-like ears and so on. Spatial relationships in portraits are very important, too; placing elements far apart or close together can change things radically. Play at being plastic surgeons or dentists, arranging features and teeth at will, and even introduce skin complaints if you want – grotesques or beauties, it's up to you.

This is exactly what a group of students from Kingston University's Illustration and Animation degree course has done (this and facing page), carving, exchanging and printing a selection of stamps to produce a whole array of characters.

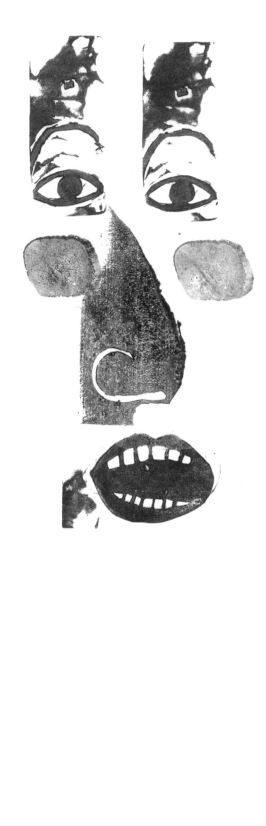

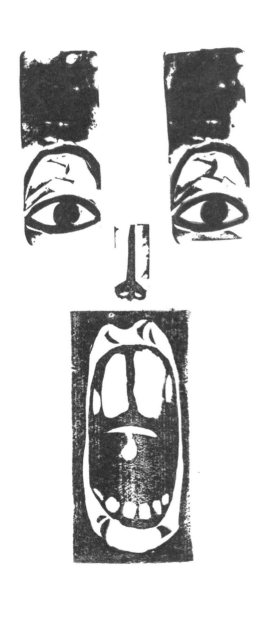

Brave new face

In 2010, Royal College of Art students Rose Blake, Mark El-khatib, Dan Frost, Paddy Molloy, Alice Moloney and Mike Redmond were invited to run a pop-up workshop creating free character portraits at the Big Chill festival, to promote Tate Britain's 'Rude Britannia' comic exhibition. They were concerned that time pressure, combined with their varied illustration styles, would lead to uneven results, so they opted instead to use rubber stamps in a few simple shapes and colours 'as a way of creating a homogenized aesthetic'. They were not only amazed at how much they managed to get out of such simple tools, but were also struck by the element of play that these introduced (this and facing page).

Playing with type

A rubber-stamp alphabet is an essential part of any stamp artist's box of tricks. Although easy to acquire (at least one will be found in every stationery or art store), contemporary sets are a little disappointing in their cut and limited choice of size and font. So why not make your own?

Creating an alphabet from scratch

You might prefer to create your own unique typeface from scratch, in which case, how do you come up with a design? Chunky block letters are common, as are characterful shadow fonts (see Edwood Burn's font on page 55), which I suspect is due to the nature of the material. In fact, this appreciation of materials is the key to creating effective rubber stamp fonts.

First of all, make a virtue of an eraser's proportions; let these determine the size and shape of your alphabet. Consider the range of erasers available, from the tiny mounds on the ends of pencils, to the jumbo 'Big Mistake' variety and the many novelty shapes available in gift stores. Allow the material itself to influence the letterform's aesthetic, too – a font stamped with a putty eraser will look remarkably different to one stamped with plastic. See John Bently's raw and immediate stamped letters (page 31), which are in direct contrast to his beautifully composed Roman graffiti-inspired fonts (overleaf, top). Carving with a range of gouging tools, will also create distinctive typefaces – see Zeel's sharp 'Demoniac Evangelist' (overleaf, bottom), or the crumbled edges of Amanda Revell's 'I moustache you a question' print (left).

Your own personality will naturally shine through, too – look at the variety of typefaces in the ransom note-style book cover created during a group workshop at the UWE's Centre for Fine Print Research (below).

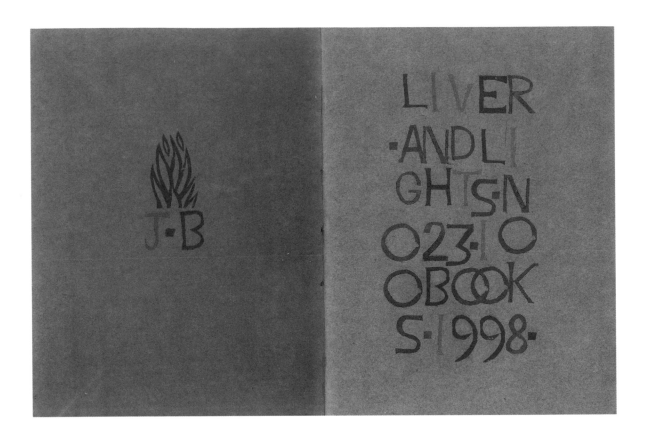

DIY alphabet stamps

You will need:

Photocopied alphabet letters (taken from typeface books or online sources)

Masking tape

A bottle of acetone, e.g. nail polish remover

Paper towel

Teaspoon

Erasers

Scalpel

The following steps show the approach used by the rubber-stamp calligrapher David Mekelburg.

Step 1. Cut out each of the photocopied letters.

Step 2. Make a start with the letter A. Cover it with an eraser and hold it in place with a piece of tape.

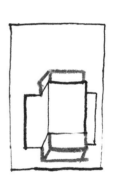

Step 3. With a little acetone on a paper towel, gently wipe the paper so that it gradually becomes transparent, taking care not to inhale the fumes.

Step 4. Transfer the letter by burnishing the back of the paper with a teaspoon.

Step 5. Now take your time and carefully carve the letter in relief. Incising a perfectly clean, sharp alphabet will be painstaking slow, but well worth it.

Movement

Traditionally, a rubber stamp's job is to print a true and clear impression. However, many rubber-stamp artists pay no heed to this convention, employing stamps as expressive mark-making tools to create prints that sing with life and movement.

Katie Hammett's print is a case in point, with gestural marks speeding around a dollar (facing page, bottom). Spatial relationships between prints are also key to creating movement, as seen in Nammi Eu's 'Cops and Robber' (facing page, top).

A stamp can also move from one side of a page to another in a flick book or stop-frame animation gif. Thomas Hicks took this approach to extremes and developed it brilliantly to make a four-minute video promo for Gravenhurst's song 'Nightwatchman's Blues' (below). Initially commissioned to make a limited-edition rubber stamp run of record sleeves, Hicks decided to make each sleeve a stop frame in an animation of the very record it was packaging.

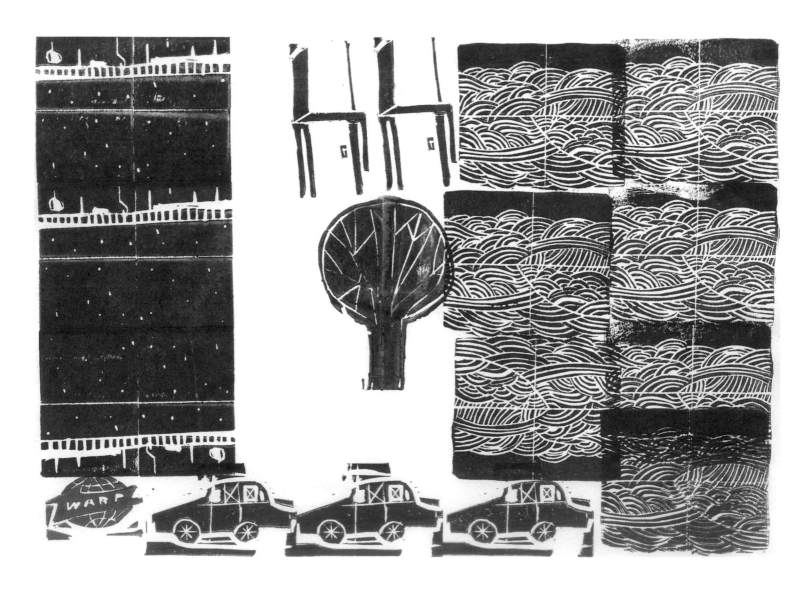

Making a thaumatrope

You will need:

White card

2 rubber stamps

Glue stick

String

Scissors

Scalpel

Why not try making your static prints move with the aid of a thaumotrope – a simple optical toy, popular in Victorian times. It consists of two images on either side of a disc; when the disc is spun, persistence of vision causes them to blur and become a single image.

Step 1. Print the first rubber stamp design (the right way up) on the sheet of card.

Step 2. Print the second rubber stamp design (upside down) on another part of the sheet of card. Cut out the two circular designs, glue them together and leave them to dry.

Step 3. Punch two holes at 9 o'clock and 3 o'clock, then feed a small length of string through each hole and tie a knot at the end to secure.

Step 4. To animate the thaumatrope, keeping the strings taut, twist them with thumb and forefingers.

Step 5. Your thaumatrope designs will magically blend into one – in this case a levitating faquir, or a moonlit pterodactyl and gentleman, as in the example opposite.

Making a thaumatrope

Overprinting

Water-based ink pads are transparent and ideal therefore for overprinting. For example, when printing yellow on top of blue you will get green, and if you layer red over blue you will get purple. Computer printers and printing presses use just four colours (cyan, magenta, yellow and black) in this way to create all the colours necessary to print any image.

While an understanding of colour theory can be very useful, I recommend supplementing any reading with plenty of practical experimentation. Begin with a simple project and playfully overlay an array of colours. Keep hold of these results and use them as a guide for future projects. With experience, you will develop an intuitive understanding of colour mixing.

Once you are feeling confident, think of a more ambitious theme that could incorporate overprinting. With a handful of stamps carved from drawings of taxidermied birds in the Bristol Museum and Art Gallery, and a roller-print cage (see overleaf) I created an aviary of tropical finches, thrushes and other birds.

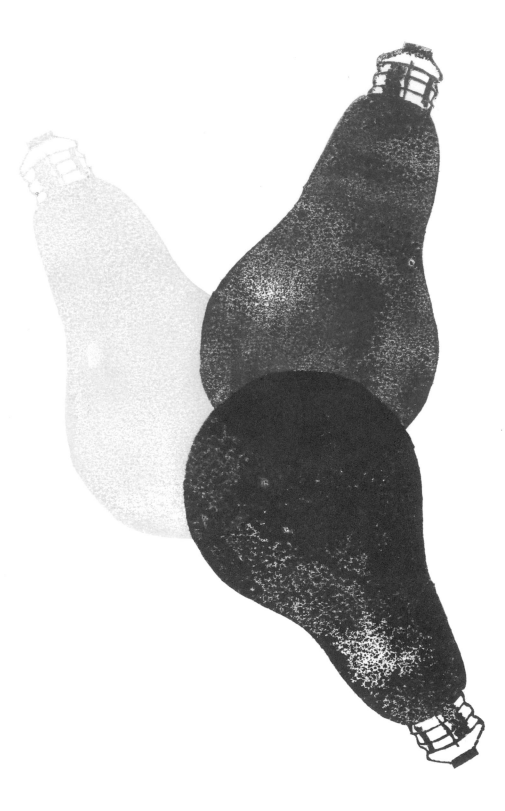

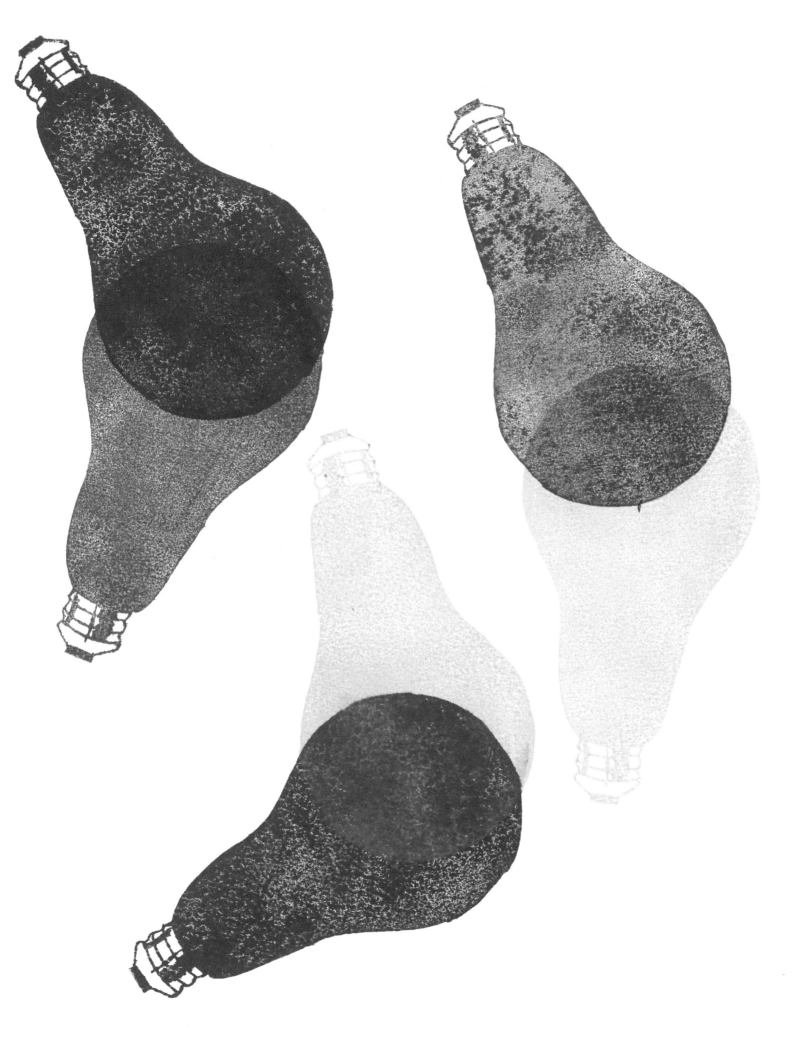

Inky colours and rubbery things

When I think of rubber stamping – the stamps themselves and the ink colours – it brings to my mind fake spiders, elastic sticky men, plastic monster masks, processed cheese, Spam, pepperoni, squares of ham and all things fake and rubbery. Combining process, media and idea to mirror the very qualities of your subject-matter gives a rubber-stamp print a rich resonance. What associations come to mind when you think of rubber stamping?

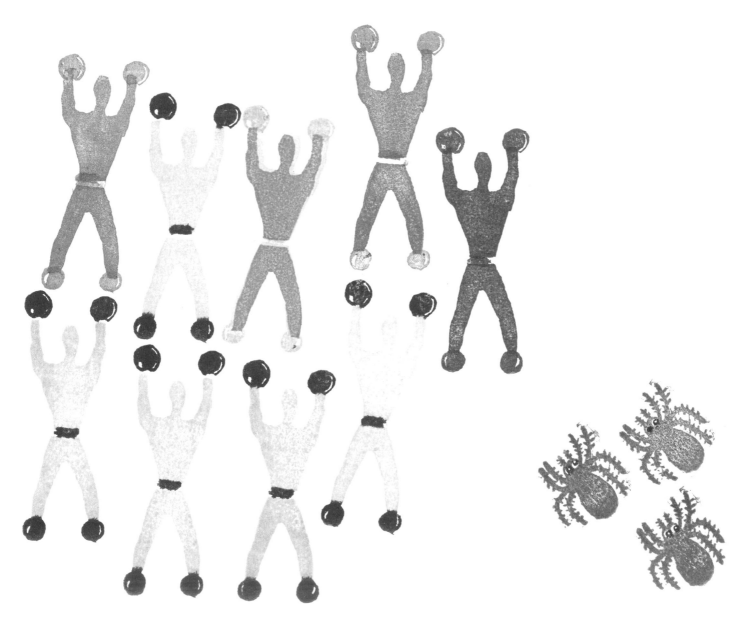

Portraits and explosions

Gather together all the rubber stamps you have used to create portraits and print them over the top of each other to see what beautiful monstrosities emerge.

Play with different colour combinations and note the effect that different tints and shades have on each other. Alternatively, carve rubber-stamp clouds of smoke, flashes and sparks, and play with inks in clashing colours to make some explosive prints.

Rainbow printing

Rainbow printing involves making a multicoloured print with a single impression by merging two or more colours on one rubber stamp. This is a simple and immediate process, which can produce captivating results. The toadstools made by a participant at a workshop at Shepherds Paper shop, London (facing page) use a toxic concoction of colours that creates a very English psychedelic resonance – a kind of Enid Blyton and Syd Barrett hybrid – while Paula Lovatt's flowers, leeks and turnips (right) are imbued with rich hues. You should of course break the rules and extend the process by printing rainbow overlays. In combining the first and second flat fish (below), the purple-headed hybrid was created.

Foam overprinting

You will need:

Craft foam sheets (available in sizes ranging from A6 to A3)

Scissors or scalpel

Water-based ink pads

Drawing utensils (try soft graphite pencils, crayons, graphite sticks and ballpoint pens)

Paper

Foam is a far more manipulative and expressive medium than rubber and, when used for overprinting, foam stamps can be coaxed into creating soft marks resembling lithographic crayon prints. As always, keep an open mind – make, play and see what happens.

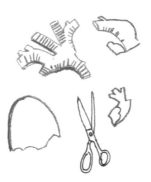

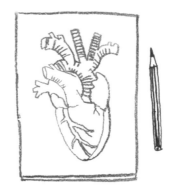

Step 1. Either draw your design on the foam before cutting or cut your design out freehand with scissors or scalpel.

Step 2. Ink up the foam pieces with different colours.

Step 3. Place the paper on top of an inked foam piece.

Step 4. Now use a pencil or crayon to scribble on the back of the paper. Vary the pressure and range of scribbled marks – try angular or circular movements, and dots and dashes.

You can even use your fingertips or fist. Pull the paper away and examine the results.

Step 5. Place the paper on another inked-up foam piece and repeat the previous step. Remove the paper and examine the results of the two overlaid colour impressions.

Step 6. Repeat Steps 4 and 5 until all the overprinting is completed.

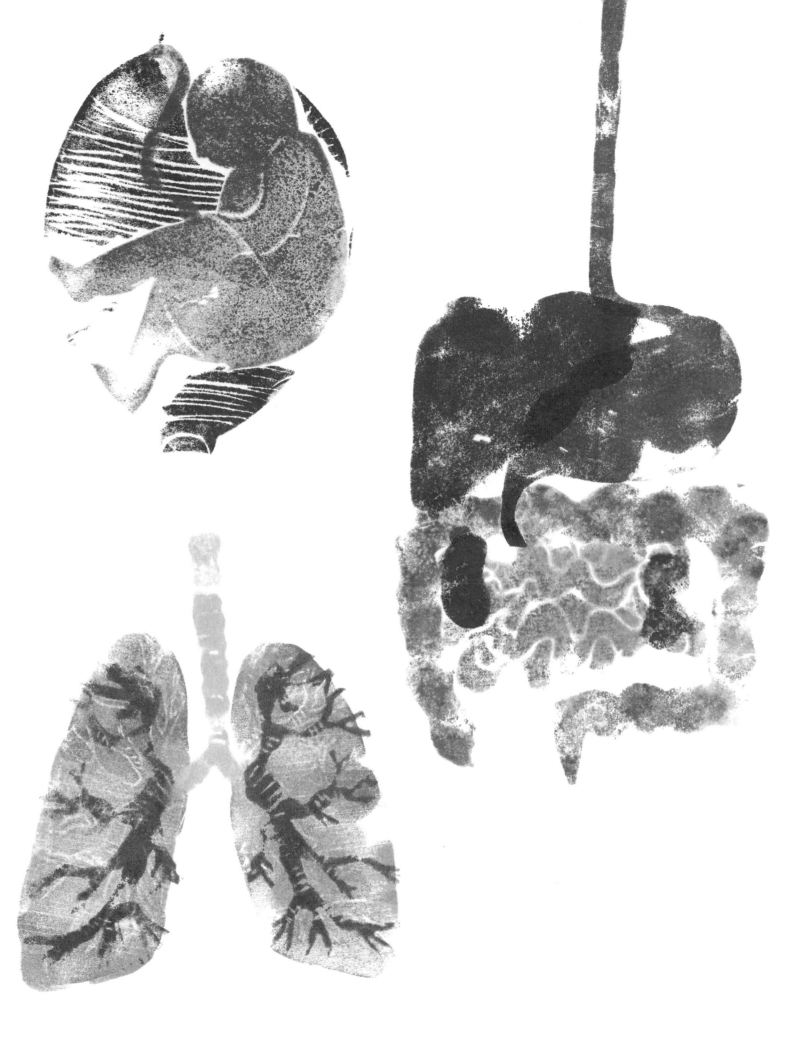

Homemade ink pads

You will need:

Foam board
Absorbent kitchen cloths
Masking tape
Drawing/airbrush inks
Brushes
Small plastic or glass vessel for
mixing the inks

**You can improvise a homemade ink
pad using just a few cheap household
materials. DIY inkpads create
very different impressions from
commercially manufactured pads.
I find that they are firm and true, with
a soft, subtle organic hue reminiscent
of watermarks, flesh tones, fruits and
sea slugs. The method shown here was
adapted from an approach devised
by the illustrator Zeel.**

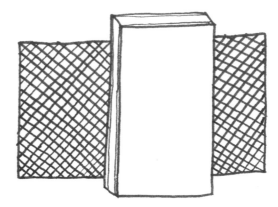

Step 1. Cut a small piece of
foam board, approximately
10 x 15 cm (4 x 6 in).

Step 2. Cut a piece of cloth
so that its width matches the
length of the foam board.

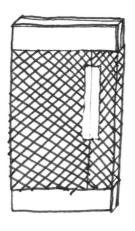

Step 3. Wrap the cloth
around the board and secure
it with masking tape.

Step 4. To colour the pad,
select an ink or mix your
own colour, then squeeze
or brush it onto the cloth.

You'll find the inks
somewhat wetter than
commercial ink pads, so be
far more gentle when inking
up your stamps – touch
rather than press them on
the pad. As the ink begins
to dry it will become tackier,
and will pick up and print
more solidly. In making one
of these makeshift pads,
you'll soon become aware
of the vast quantity of
ink that is pumped into
a commercial version!

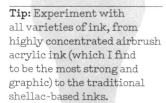

Tip: Experiment with
all varieties of ink, from
highly concentrated airbrush
acrylic ink (which I find
to be the most strong and
graphic) to the traditional
shellac-based inks.

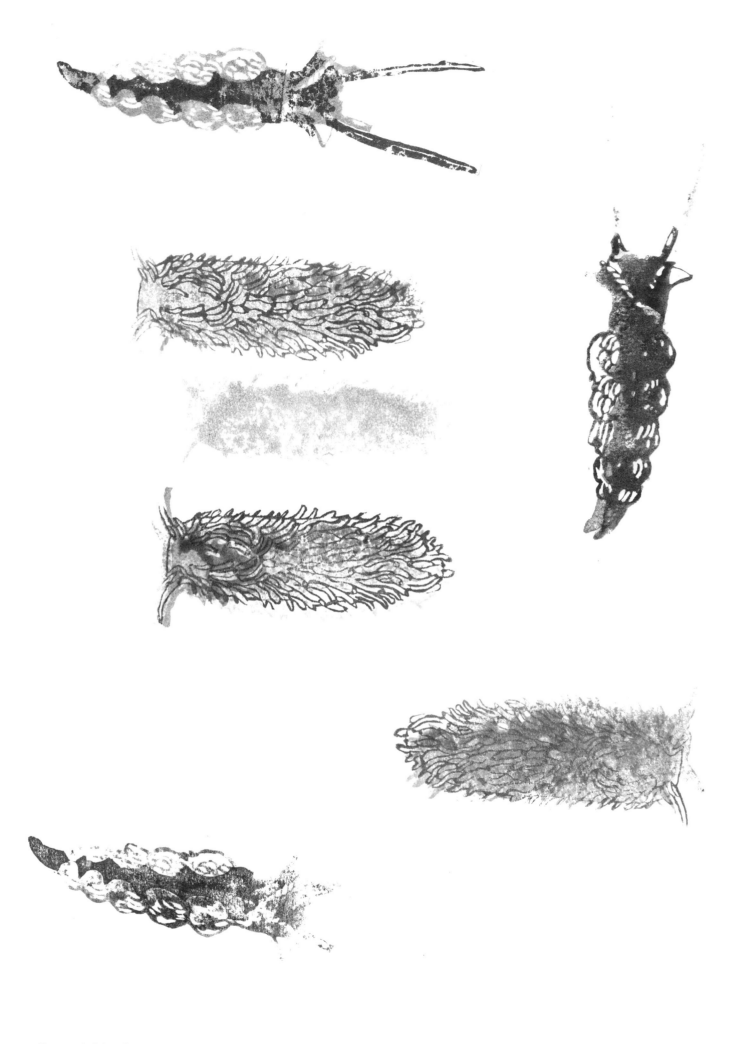

Printing with bleach

You will need:

200 gsm cartridge paper
Drawing board
Water
Large household paintbrush
Gummed brown tape
Coloured ink
Thick bleach gel
Small glass jar (for safety, labelled 'bleach')
Rubber stamps
Small paintbrush with synthetic bristles
Rubber gloves

My artist's book Cosmic Forces is an exploration of 1930s and '40s American B movies and their fascination with séances and mediums. These films used the props of spiritualism – darkened rooms, ouija boards, floating spirit hands and ectoplasm – to convey the strange and the 'other', and to spook the audience in the process. By printing with bleach you, too, can conjure up ghostly figures 'from the vasty deep'.

Step 1. Start by stretching the paper. Use the large brush to apply plenty of water to the both sides of the paper. Let the paper soak up the liquid, making sure it's completely wet through. Leave the paper on the drawing board.

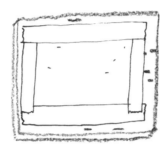

Step 2. Wet the gummed tape and apply it along all the edges of the wet paper and board. Leave to dry completely.

Step 3. Apply a coat of coloured ink (I used an old bottle of red ink).

Step 4. Pour a small amount of bleach into your jar, then paint a thin layer of it over your rubber stamp.

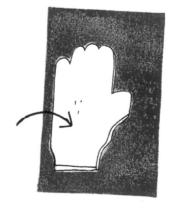

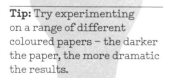

Tip: Try experimenting on a range of different coloured papers – the darker the paper, the more dramatic the results.

Step 5. Press the bleach-covered stamp on the inked paper. Printing on dry ink will create a crisp impression; if you print on wet ink the impression will bleed, leaving a much softer edge.

Step 6. Clean the rubber stamp with plenty of water.

Step 7. To create the appearance of a spirit body, use the same stamp to print an uneven ink impression over the bleach print.

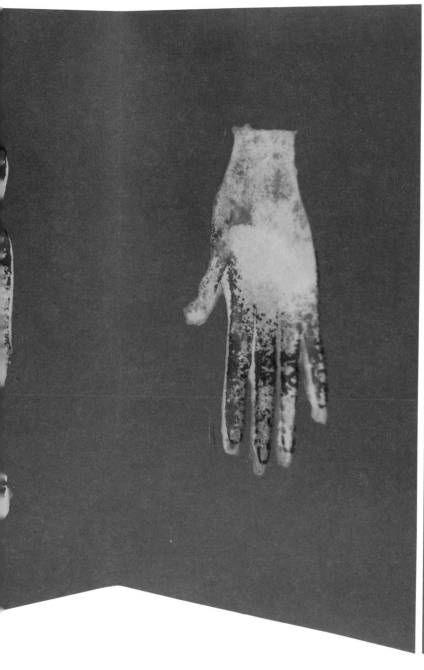

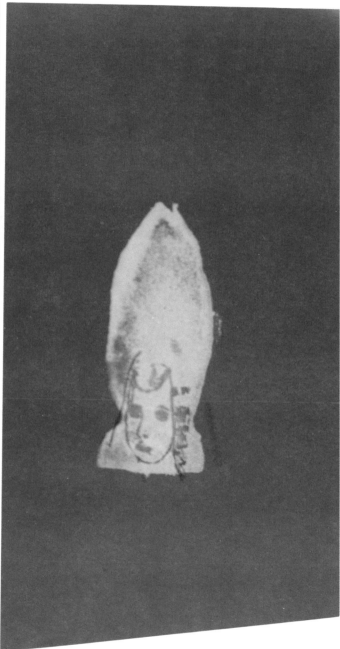

Ghost postcards

Stamped ghosts can haunt old
postcards and photographs,
transforming them into new works.
The majority of white ink pads produce
frustratingly translucent results,
but you can take advantage of their
shortcomings as ink pads to create
impressions of lost souls wandering
along cloisters and through walls.

Prior Bolton's Window.

South Ambulatory.

Tomb of Rahere, the Founder of the Church and the Hospital.

Interventions: printing on the body

Printing on the body is an exciting performance, shared by the stamper and the stamped. Put your paper away and start printing on flesh – it's like nothing else.

Print on your girlfriend, boyfriend, wife, husband, friend, next-door neighbour or boss. Make your stamping a private affair – re-enact the rubber-stamping scene in the film Closely Watched Trains – or arrange an event for public consumption.

Make faces red without embarrassment! Not hairy enough? Easily solved. Or give yourself a pretend black eye, a temporary tattoo, freckles or spots.

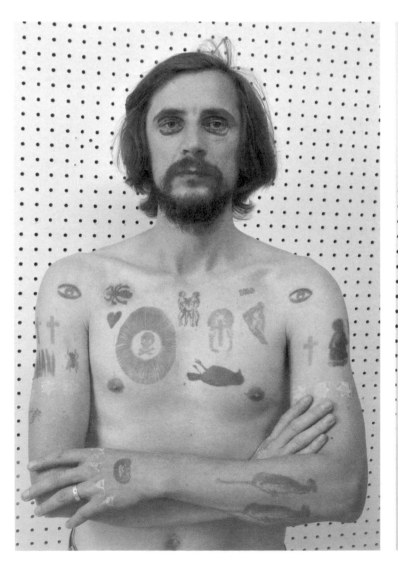

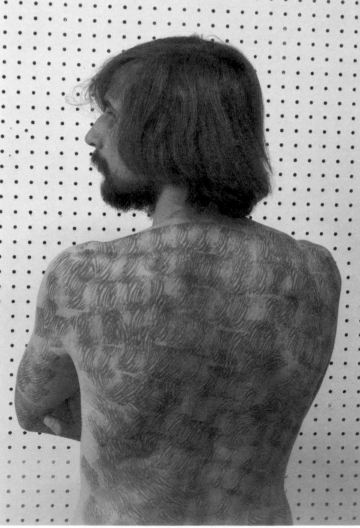

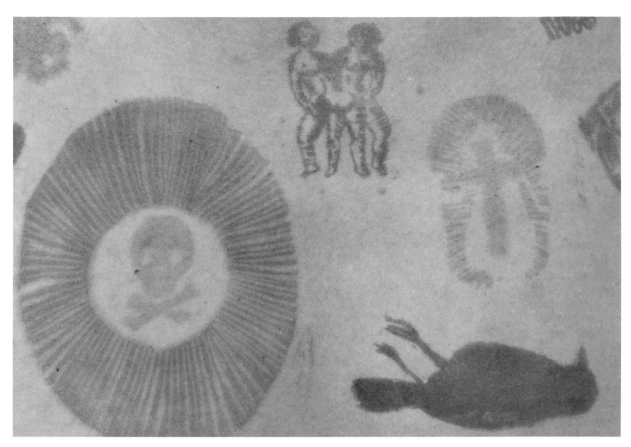

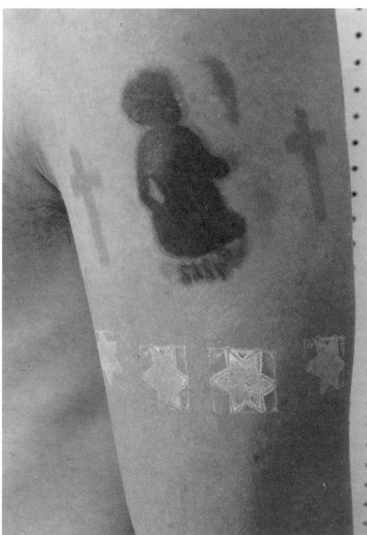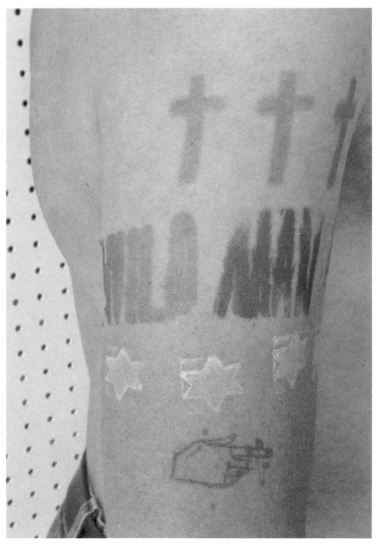

Interventions: printing in public

Printing in public – aka graffiti – offers another outlet for the rubber stamper. As Joni Miller and Lowry Thompson put it in The Rubber Stamp Album, 'Defacing public monuments – in a nice way, of course – can be as easy as putting stamps in your pocket. There is no point in leaving home without at least one or two whose sole purpose is to save you the trouble of drawing a moustache or a pair of lips.'

Gather a random selection of stamps and a few ink pads for your first trip. Scatter your stamps indiscriminately at first, allowing for happy accidents. Enjoy seeing your creations climbing up walls or appearing in adverts, transforming these contexts. Soon you will discover new possibilities and start planning for forthcoming trips, perhaps even carving new stamps for the purpose.

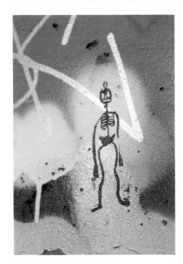

David Lemm (this page) explored the notion of public printing in an interactive event he devised in Edinburgh in 2014. Participants were given a print depicting a route, along which were locations where a rubber stamp and ink pad stood waiting. Each custom-made stamp featured a symbol related to its surroundings, and participants followed the trail, using the stamps to record their experience of the route by completing their own version of the print.

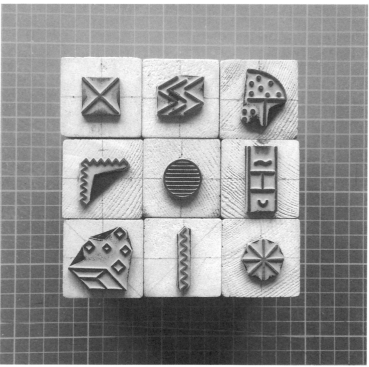

Playing with officialdom

One of the first stamps that many people will carve will be a word, a phrase or even their own name – a graffiti tag that says 'I was here'. This desire to make a personal mark on your surroundings is akin to the basic urge to carve a name into a tree.

Making your own type also gives a sense of authority, based on the experience that rubber stamps tell us clearly when a library book is due or when food is out of date, and allow us access to nightclubs and foreign countries! Think about identification and numbering and make a set of stamps that communicate with an air of officialdom. Your message will be perceived very differently from a handwritten note or typed text.

from a garden

CERTIFIED

Public

THANK YOU

NO THANK YOU

THIS IS...
FUN

A
BIT
SILLY

SCRAP

PAID

SAUCE

MADE UP

Religious Article

things from a Pocket

Mail art

It's hard to sum up mail art in a single sentence. It is a process rather than a product, and it involves people of all ages and backgrounds who exchange not only printed material but also a wide range of works (including sculpture and music) through the post.

Rubber stamping is highly suited to mail art. A project will twist and turn, with rubber stamp 'tags' identifying each contributor's handiwork as the work loops between sender and recipient. Intertwined among this are franking marks, postmarks and stamped commands of 'DO NOT BEND' – the official visual language of the postal system.

Create new stamps for the occasion or delve into your archive: old stamps will be reinvigorated and reinterpreted by the stamps that accompany them on the envelope.

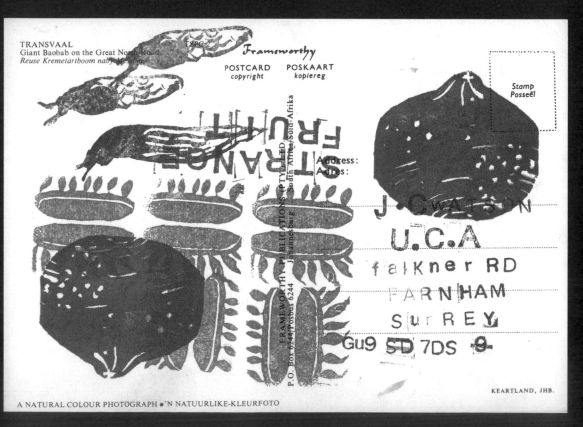

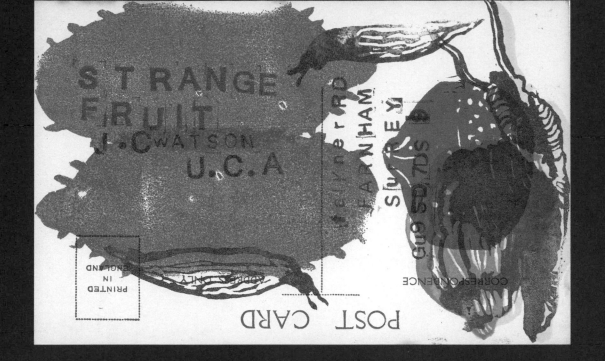

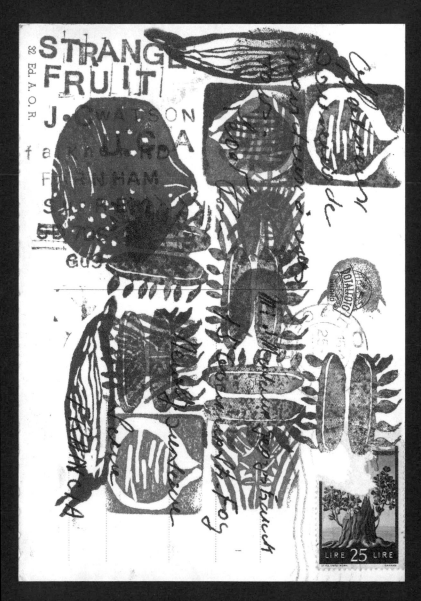

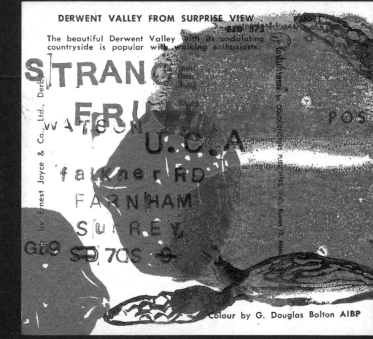

Joining a network

Make a simple start by exchanging mail art with a distant friend. To Jo Cook (aka Bucky Fleur) I sent rubber-stamped dinosaur postcards, which I collaborated on with Rei Archer, and a joyful and colourful response was sent back in turn. John Bently's post to me (overleaf) was a surprise, featuring stamps from his archive – including a fornicating pair of rabbits. This I duly returned, with the addition of their offspring, and the offspring's offspring.

Take things a step further by creating a network with a small group of friends. This will have the potential of extending into a wider group of mail-art associates. Initiate introductions of friends of friends and let it spread over the world.

You may also send mail art as a one-way activity: as protest, encouragement or as gifts, for example the 'Strange Fruit' series, made for a University of the University of the Creative Arts, Farnham Illustration course publication (featured on pages 88–9).

Finally, joining an international mail-art network can bring you the freedom of anonymity and allow you to take more playful risks. (See the back of the book for addresses.)

Keep any mail-art exchange as simple as possible, at least at first; complicated projects end up frustrating all concerned. Once a relationship has started, a rhythm or structure will naturally emerge and a project will soon develop a life of its own.

Bucky Fleur
410 Bowsprit Crescent
Mayne Island, B.C CANADA
VON2J2

ALTERED

THE ADDRESS TO BE WRITTEN

Stephen Fowler
390 a Hackney Road

London U.K.

E2 7AP

par avion

Royal Mail®

Bucky Fleur
410 Bowsprit Crescent
Mayne Island, B.C. CANADA
VoN 2J2

TO

Stephen Fowler

390a Hackney Road

London U.K.
E2 7AP

LONDON
SE24 OLX

1ST
Large

TO
NERVOUS STEPHEN
390A HACKNEY RD
LONDON
E2 7AP

1st Large
up to 100g
006009.1-38414-03

FROM
john BENTLY
229 RaiLTon RD

Sender: McLennon, Wismije, CH435 TZ

Artistamps

Artistamps, or artist's stamps, are closely associated with mail art: they reflect its spirit of marrying art and the everyday. Stamps signify payment, and mail artists test and tease the postal system with their playful appropriation of this official form of evidence.

I enjoy the challenge of trying to replicate a perforated sticky-backed sheet of machine-made stamps, but there are no right or wrong ways to make artistamps.

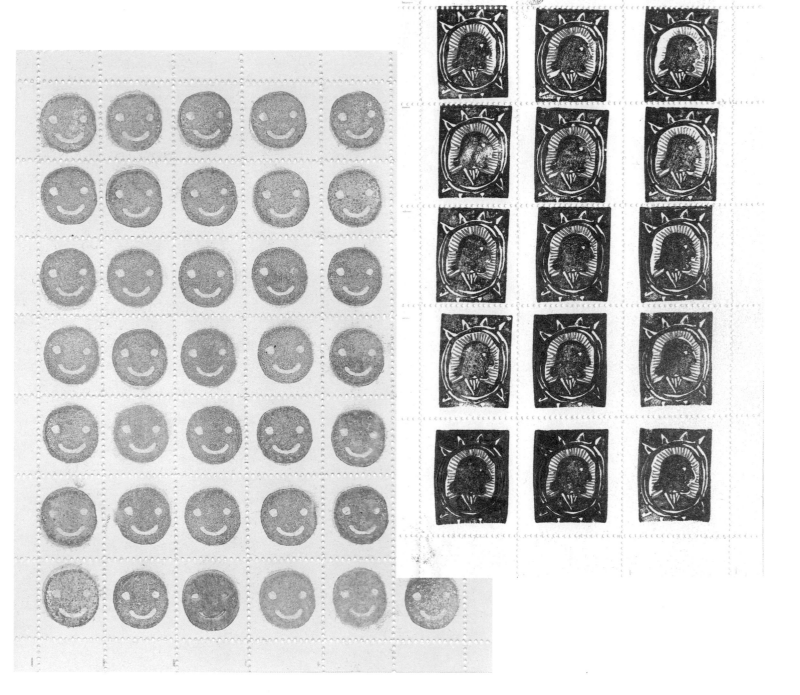

Cinderella stamps

A Cinderella stamp is any stamp produced outside the auspices of a governmental postal system. Mail artists have long printed stamps of imaginary lands and authorities. Heathcote Williams and Richard Adams, for example, produced a 'God Will Provide' stamp dedicated to the 'Free Independent Republic of Frestonia', a London street that attempted to declare itself independent from the British Isles in the 1970s. And, of course, many a mail artist seeks the thrill of accidental endorsement by the postal system.

Brainstorming led me to thoughts of acid blotter stamps, and to Arthur Ransome's children's novel Pigeon Post (below right). I also began to play with silly puns, such as 'stamp!' (right) and some pink 'mail' men (below left) – look carefully and you'll notice the pink musclebound men checking each other out.

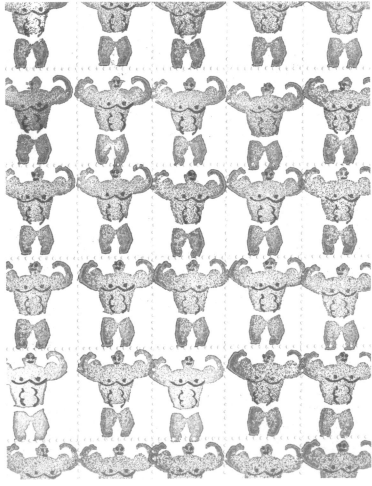

Perforations

Step 1. At one end of the tube, sharpen the outside edges with the file.

You will need:

2.5 cm (1 in) of ⅛ in hollow brass tubing
Small metal file
Scalpel
Card stock
Sewing-machine
Iron

I am lucky to have access to a large foot-operated perforating machine in a friendly school art department. If you ask politely, and perhaps offer a small donation, some postal museums will allow their perforating machines to be put to use. John Held Jr, mail-art expert and collector, also offers a perforating service via his PO-box address, with the proviso that he keeps one of every ten stamp sheets perforated. Or use Kula Moku's ingenious sewing-machine solution described here.

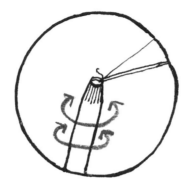

Step 2. Sharpen the inside edges with the scalpel. Hold the scalpel at a 45-degree angle and swivel the tubing clockwise, then anti-clockwise, producing small brass peelings.

Step 3. Replace the sewing-machine needle with the sharp brass tubing.

Tip: You can also try piercing stamp sheets with an overstitch wheel or rotary perforator, guided along the edge of a metal ruler. This won't create the classic perforated dots, but will still produce perfectly usable tear lines.

Step 4. Place several pieces of card stock under your sheet of stamps and then carefully 'sew' through the paper and card to leave cleanly cut perforations.

Step 5. Iron the sheet of stamps so it's nice and flat.

Rubber-stamped ephemera

Rubber stamps were designed as a simple, economical way to create official forms of signage, and they offer democratized graphic solutions to all manner of ventures: instructions, insignia, warnings and labels.

Visit haberdashers, kitchenware stores, stationers or chemists with your 'rubber-stamp glasses' on. Tags, stickers (such as the ones by Zeel, far right), beer mats, bookmarks, paper plates, postcards, toilet rolls, badges, plasters, paper planes or matchboxes (such as Helen Allesbrook's, far right) can also provide a starting point for a piece of art. Transcend context, subvert playfully – make people smile or see things in a new light.

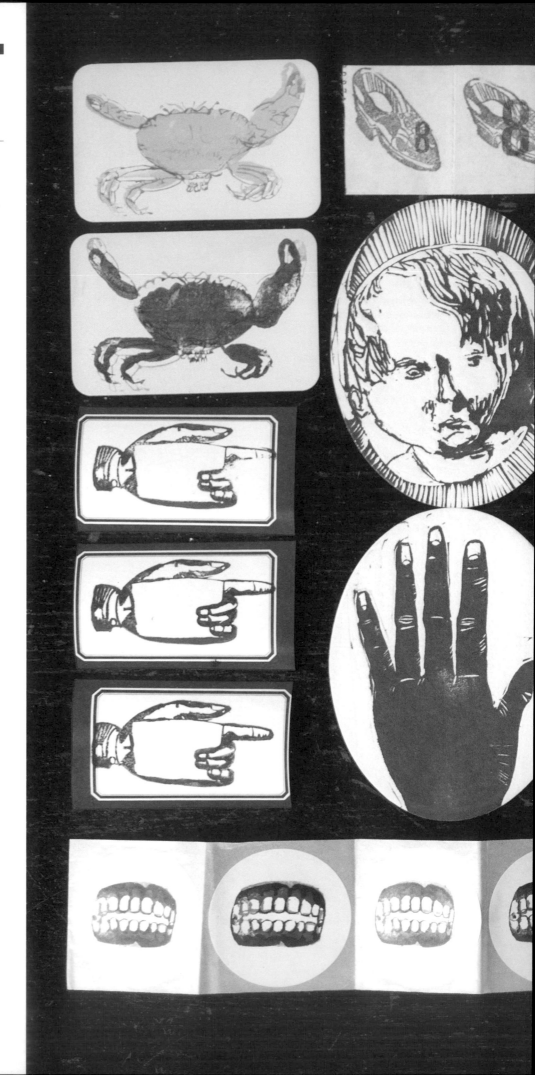

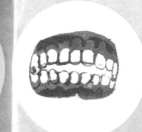

Gigantic stamps

If you think you've exhausted the possibilities of rubber stamps then it's time to move on to large stamps! Take a look at Vincent Sardon's beautifully absurd ginormous rubber stamps for inspiration.

Always keep loose change in your pocket in case you spot a large novelty eraser – they show up in the most unexpected places. Japanese Radar erasers come in a range of sizes, from a satisfyingly palm-sized model up to a gigantic 28 x 14 x 43 cm (11 x 5 ½ x 17 in), with an equally hefty price tag. A cheaper alternative is the pink Speedy-Carve block by US brand Speedball, which goes up to 30 x 30 cm (12 x 12 in), or the Soft-Kut eraser, which reaches 30 x 45 cm (12 x 18 in).

By far the cheapest option is the craft foam sheets. These come in A3 size and can be doubled up on large pieces of wood for an even bigger stamp. Zeel's preference is for packing foam, which is both chunky and easy to manoeuvre – see the results in his flower print (overleaf). He has developed this distinctive approach to printing on fabric, making t-shirts, armband patches and large back jacket patches for his invented band, Pigswool.

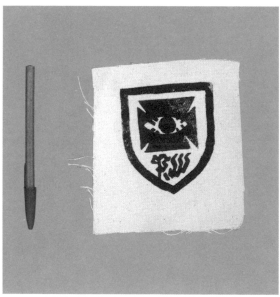

Rubber stamps on handles

Both erasers and foam stamps can be mounted on wood or thick board and then given handles for better grip and swifter stamping. Hardware stores and flea markets will have an array of handles to choose from. Game counters offer a quirky alternative: small chess pawns are excellent for little stamps, since they can be held neatly between thumb and forefinger.

Most rubber–stamp materials are soft and cushiony by nature and will 'give' enough when printing to make a clear image. Harder materials like Soft–Kut will need a foam-sheet layer between the stamp and handle.

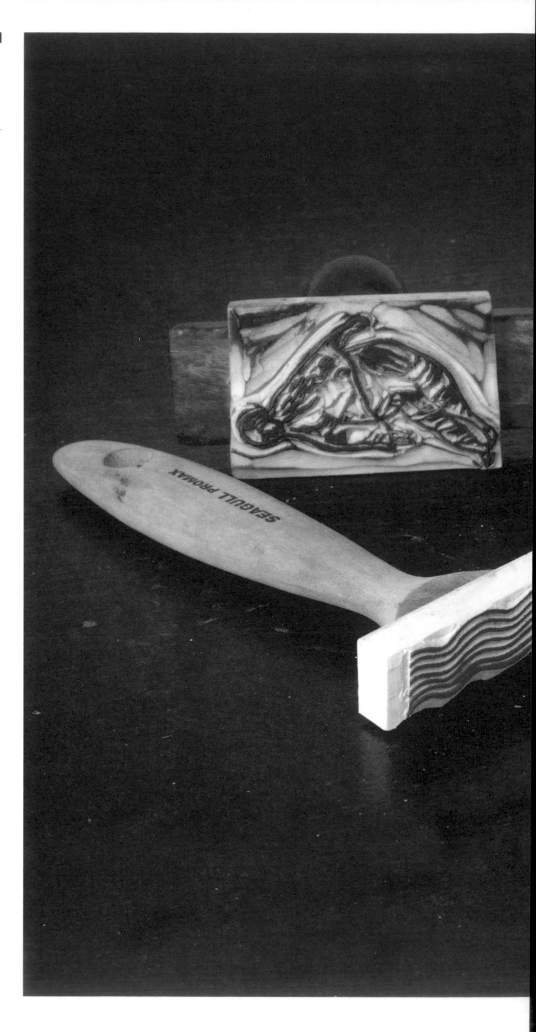

Edible prints

As Joni Miller and Lowry Thompson point out in **The Rubber Stamp Album**, 'At a certain point in stamp consciousness, merely stamping paper becomes old hat and you'll suspiciously start eyeing other likely surfaces with a wild gleam in your eye.' When this happens, you will almost certainly turn your attention to food.

Rubber stamp pigments are available that can be used to print on meat and eggs, but these are not suitable for human consumption. If you want to produce edible stamped food you need to use thick food dye. A new pad will be required for every colour.

Make sure you wash your hands and your stamps thoroughly before you start, and treat your stamps with a sterilizing liquid. It is also best to avoid stamps that have any small incisions where bacteria can fester.

Tip: Why not use rubber stamps to decorate your cookies and cakes? The flatter the surface, the better the print. Make sure that your frosting or icing is completely dry before printing. Royal icing is ideal for printing!

Rubber-stamp buildings

You will need:

Pencil

Metal ruler

Thin card

Architectural/textured rubber stamps

Scalpel

Cutting mat

Bone folder

Coloured ink pads

Glue stick

This simple project has been devised to introduce you to the potential of three-dimensional rubber stamping. Have a go at making this simple building, then move on to more elaborate designs of your own.

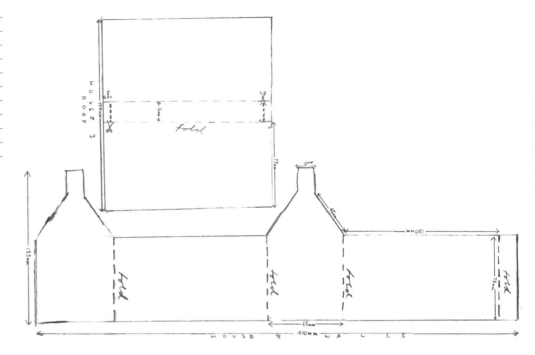

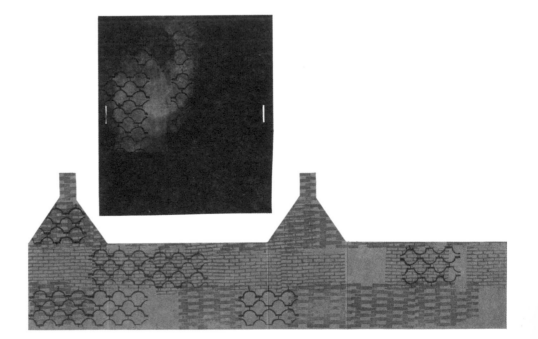

Step 1. Using the pencil and ruler, draw out the components of your structure on card; use the diagram as a guide. The dimensions can be adjusted according to the desired outcome – a square box for a simple two-storey house, perhaps, or an elongated rectangle for an apartment block.

Step 2. Using your stamps, print the architectural details on the front, back, sides and roof.

Step 3. With a scalpel and metal ruler carefully cut out each element.

Step 4. Using the ruler and bone folder, score along the dividing lines and tabs.

Step 5. To finish, fold the flat pieces into a box and glue the corresponding tabs together.

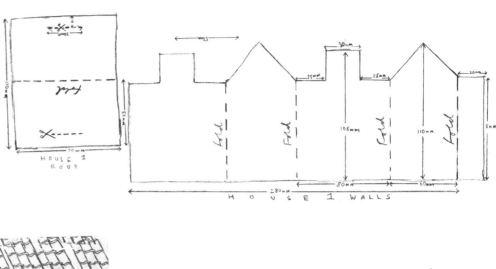

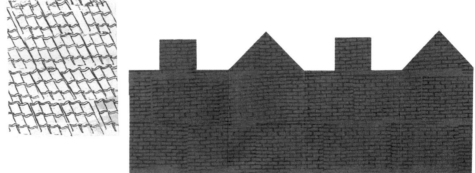

Rubber-stamp leftovers

Stampers will soon accumulate plenty of eraser leftovers, chopped off or carved away through the making of many a rubber stamp. I have boxes of them.

Don't let these leftovers go to waste – ink them up and 'draw' with them instead. Think mosaics, shell grottos and rock gardens. Here is what I did with mine. What will you print with yours?

ALTERNATIVE PRINT METHODS

The aim of this chapter is to capture the inventive spirit of the many books devised by printmakers and teacher training departments in the 1960s and '70s to introduce teachers to craft processes in an accessible way. This attitude of freedom and inclusivity encouraged readers to develop upon what they read, unbound by orthodox methods.

Here, then, you'll find a selection of simple processes such as plaster and clay printing, together with exercises and diagrams to help you get to grips with each one. I have also included instructions for those interested in reproducing artwork in the form of simple books. Whatever your level, my hope is that this chapter will leave you wanting to make, make, make.

Roller printing

In 1961 the English-born poet, painter and subversive Brion Gysin created a simple printing tool by adapting a rubber paint roller, incising it with thin overlapping lines. This DIY process is both economical and highly addictive.

Once you've carved and printed several roller designs, it's worth reflecting on your results. I tend to print my designs in straight lines, taking great care to make evenly inked impressions. Other roller printers work very differently.

Many use a roller much more freely, making circular stretched looped prints, to create the effect of large, elongated blown bubbles, while children enjoy running the length of a room, with an outstretched arm running a roller along a papered wall.

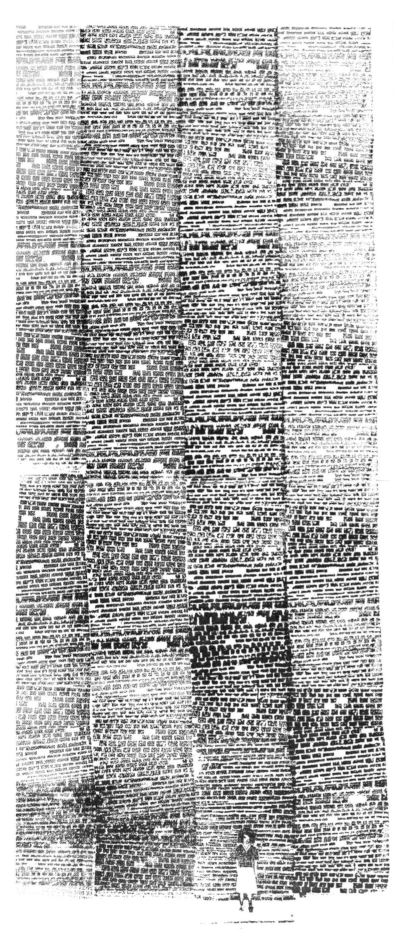

Think about printing direction. Vertical patterns like Danny Stanton's clever night-time car repeat (facing page) or these brick motifs can be joined together to make an awesomely high wall, or split at different heights to suggest towers and chimneys. Adding a figure at the bottom will add a sense of scale.

Continuous rolled repeats can be explored horizontally, too. They were used to create the imaginative 'Endless Landscapes' shown on pages 120–1.

This landscape was printed using black Ocaldo watercolour ink with five interchangeable carved rollers, representing sky, landforms, trees, tree trunks and houses. The foam lagging gently repelled the water-based ink for a subtle marble-like effect, and overlays of different densities of ink contributed to the final, hazy mirage of a landscape.

Of course, you can also combine horizontally and vertically themed rollers to great effect. Children don't abide by any conventions and so come up with all sorts of exciting diagonal, curved and overlaid outcomes. Printmaker Chloe Alexander's beautiful multilayered prints (below) resonate with the same kind of enthusiastic energy.

Making an adapted roller

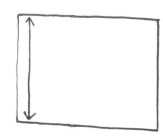

For a small roller you will need:

A mini paint roller, around 20 mm
(¾ in) in diameter

Pipe lagging with a 20 mm (¾ in)
internal diameter

For a large roller you will need:

A large paint roller, around 50 mm
(2 in) in diameter

Protective scaffolding foam with
a 50 mm (2 in) internal diameter

You will also need:

Pencil

Scalpel

Metal ruler

A4 (8 x 11½ in) sheet of paper

Masking tape

Scissors

Scotch Magic tape

UHU glue

Cheap water-based relief-printing ink

Ink roller and block

Wallpaper lining paper

**Fashion your own roller by manipulating
pipe lagging or scaffolding foam. Both
are easy to carve, fit neatly around a
paint roller, and they transfer ink well.**

Step 1. Cut a piece of
lagging/foam to the same
length as your paint roller.
Using the scalpel and metal
ruler, cut a strip of paper
to the same length.

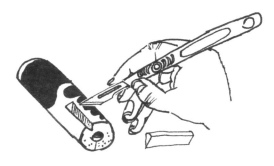

Step 5. Now attach your
paper pattern to the tube.
Most lagging/foam comes
with a pre-made slit or cut-
line indentation, so to avoid
any interference with the
design, stick the paper next
to this slit with masking
tape, curl the rest of the
paper around, and stick it
down with more tape. The
tube is ready for carving.

Step 6. Holding the scalpel
like a pencil, pierce the
paper and the lagging/foam
and cut along the outside of
the design, carving one side
of a V-shape, before turning
the tube round and carving
the other side of the V-shape.
Make sure the cuts meet
at the bottom – a V-shaped
length of foam should pop out
easily. If this proves tricky,

your scalpel is probably
blunt. Replace it with a new
blade and try again. Keep
the Magic tape at the ready
to stick any troublesome
peeling paper in place.

Tip: Compared to conventional
relief printing, a considerable
amount of ink is needed to
create a good adapted-roller
print, so experiment with
cheap water-based relief-
printing ink to begin with.

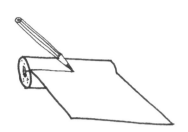
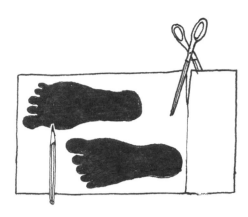

Step 2. Attach one end of the paper strip to the tube with masking tape; curl the rest of paper around the lagging/foam.

Step 3. Mark where the paper overlaps with a pencil line.

Step 4. Detach the paper from the tube, and trim to size along the pencil line. Now draw your design in pencil or pen. As this is a tubular relief-printing process, spread the design evenly across the paper, as this will prevent any carved areas touching the ink during the inking-up stage. Remember, too, that your design will print in reverse, so carve any text or numerals accordingly.

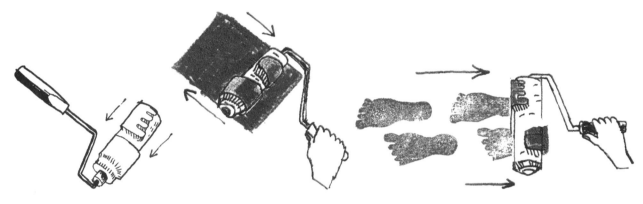

Step 7. Now slide the foam tube onto the paint roller. If your carved tube is of the pre-slit variety, seal it with UHU glue. You are now ready for inking up.

Step 8. Squeeze a dollop of relief-printing ink onto the ink block and use the ink roller to spread it out to around 1mm in thickness, and wide enough for your roller. Gently roll your adapted roller back and forth across the ink without applying any pressure; make sure the foam is completely covered before attempting your first print.

Step 9. Attach several lengths of wallpaper lining paper to a wall, table or floor. Place the adapted roller at the top of your paper and roll downwards. For a consistent print, apply pressure in relation to the quantity of ink – start with very little pressure and gradually apply more force until you're out of ink.

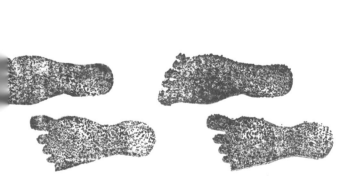

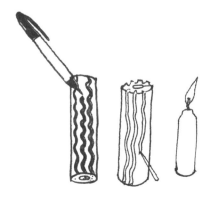

Tip: Bypass paper and draw straight onto the foam with a permanent marker. Alternatively, try heating a large needle over a candle flame and use the hot needle to carve into the foam. This is a superb way of creating detail.

Roller postcards and books

One of the strengths of roller printing is its speed of reproduction. In an instant, three good repeats can be produced from one inked-up roller; cut them into separate pieces and you've got a small print edition. This is faster than many automated printing presses.

A simple place to start is by making a series of postcards. You can either tape down a number of blank postcards, neck to neck, or simpler still, you can use one long piece of card and cut it up later. Ink up your roller and run it along the length of card(s).

One-sheet concertina books

You will need:

A length of wallpaper lining paper – approx. 1 metre (3ft long)
Large paint roller
Small paint roller
Numerous carved scaffolding-foam tubes and pipe-lagging tubes
Relief-printing inks
Ink roller and block
Masking tape
Bone folder

Select a piece of paper that is substantial enough to take a few layers of roller ink. I prefer a length of wallpaper lining paper, around 1 metre (3 ft) long.

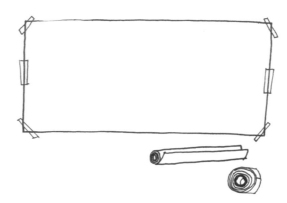

Step 1. Reverse roll the paper to make it sit flat, then attach it to a work surface or wall with masking tape.

Step 2. Use a limited range of colours and a few carved tubes to create your design. With this overlay method there's no need to wait for colours to dry between coats.

Step 3. When the print is completely dry, fold the length of paper in half horizontally.

Step 4. Now fold the length of paper in half again so that you have something resembling a greetings card.

Step 5. Peel back one side of this 'card' so that it meets the spine and fold again.

Step 6. Flip the 'card' over and repeat step 5 to complete your book.

One-sheet instant books

You will need:

A multi-layered roller print (any size/dimensions of paper)

Bone folder

Scissors/scalpel

Metal ruler

This couldn't be easier: take a piece of roller printed paper (any size will do, from A3 to a length of wallpaper lining), fold it, make a single cut and hey presto – a book. See page 128 for an example of an instant book.

Step 1. Fold the paper in half lengthways.

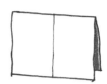

Step 2. Open it up, then fold the paper horizontally.

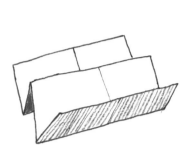

Step 3. Fold each end of the paper back to the middle, so you have a concertina, zigzag fold.

Step 4. Cut down the middle section.

Step 5. Open the paper up and fold it over so that the sheet is in the long horizontal folded position again.

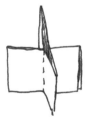

Step 6. Push the sides towards each other to form a T-shape.

Step 7. Gather and fold all the sections together, making a traditional book form.

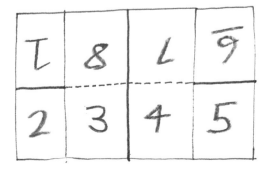

Tip: The page order of an instant book can be improvised, or planned according to an instant-book structure: on the bottom of the sheet (left to right) pages 2, 3, 4 and 5. Above these, and upside down (right to left) pages 6, 7, 8 and 1.

Single-section books

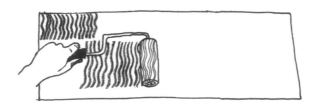

You will need:

Wallpaper lining paper – approx.
1 meter x 25 cm (3ft long x 9 inches)
Large paint roller
Small paint roller
Numerous carved scaffolding-foam tubes
and pipe-lagging tubes
Relief-printing inks
Ink roller and block
Masking tape
Bone folder
Awl
Linen thread and bookbinding needle
Binder clip
Scalpel
Metal Ruler

This method has been devised without taking the final order of the book's pages into account, allowing for surprising juxtapositions to appear in the bound book.

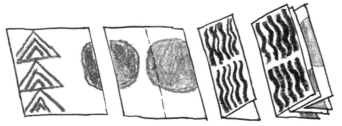

Step 2. Do the same on the other side of the paper. Leave to dry.

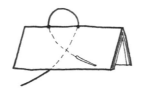

Step 3. Cut the paper into three equal sections, fold them in half and gather them together.

Step 4. Using the awl, punch three holes in the book's spine: near the top, in the middle and near the bottom. Next pass a threaded needle through the second hole and first hole of the book.

Step 5. Now pass the needle and thread through the third hole.

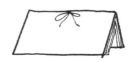

Step 6. Then go back again through the second hole.

Step 7. Secure the thread with a knot.

Edritioned single-section books

You will need:

3 sheets of A3 scrap paper

3 sheets of A3 paper (approx. 150 gsm) per booklet.

Large paint roller

Small paint roller

Numerous carved scaffolding foam tubes and pipe-lagging tubes

Relief-printing inks

Ink roller and block

Scotch magic tape

Bone folder

Awl

Linen thread and bookbinding needle

Binder clip

Scalpel

Metal Ruler

Pencil

**This approach is ideal for printing large editions of booklets. Each A3 sheet of paper will make four pages, so three A3 sheets will produce an A4 12-page booklet. To work out how many sheets of paper you will need for your print run, decide on your edition number and multiply by three.
See page 130–31 for an example of pages printed this way.**

Step 1. Make a mock-up of your booklet to plan its page sequence. Fold the three sheets of the scrap paper in half, making an A4 book. Quickly draw the contents, number the pages 1 to 12, then separate it out into three sheets of paper again to use as a visual guide for printing.

Step 2. Start by printing all the sheets corresponding to the pages numbers 1 (cover) and 12 (back cover) on one side of the paper, and pages 2 and 11 on the other. To print the cover, place the sheets on top of each other, overlapping every front cover with the back cover. Hold them in place on your work surface with Magic tape. Ink up and print your design/image/text, rolling across three or four covers, or until the ink runs out. Repeat until all the covers are printed, then leave them to dry.

Step 3. Next, print the back cover. Place all the back covers so they overlap the front covers, hold in place with Magic tape. As before, print, then leave to dry.

Step 4. Repeat the same process for the back of all the sheets (such as pages 2 and 11). Then do the same for all the front pages of the booklet.

Step 5. Collate the loose printed pages, creating a batch of 12-page booklets. Check the page sequence before binding with the three-hole pamphlet stitch used in the previous exercise.

Tip: To save time, print your sheets in a strategic sequence. While the cover is drying, prepare the sheet containing pages 3, 10, 4 and 9. Overlap page 3 with page 10 and print the desired page 3 design. While this page is drying, prepare the sheet containing pages 5, 6, 7 and 8, and print pages 6 and 7. Continue until all the sheets are printed.

The Rant Mullins Bigfoot project

You will need:

A2 sheet of 2 mm grey board
Sheet of blue upholstery foam, approx 50 x 50 x 0.5 cm (20 x 20 x ¼ in)
Scissors
Craft knife
Pencil
Marker pen
Heavy-duty multi-purpose spray adhesive
Velcro
Relief-printing ink
Ink roller and block
Paper

Bigfoot is a creature said to live in the forests of North America. Despite numerous reported sitings, a retired logger called Rant Mullins came forward in the 1980s and confessed to having carved a giant pair of feet in 1930 and used them to produce footprints as a practical joke.

Whilst not wanting to encourage a sceptical attitude towards Bigfoot in any way, I took inspiration from Mr Mullins's ingenuity and made my own pair of Bigfoot foam feet for a printing workshop at Margate's Turner Contemporary 'Curiosity' exhibition.

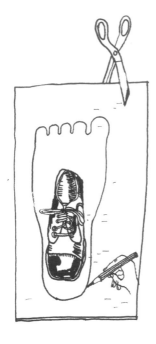
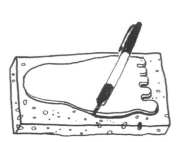
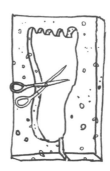

Step 1. Start by drawing an outline of Bigfoot's left foot – around 35 cm (14 in) long and 15 cm (6 in) wide, to match Mullins's originals – on the grey board. Cut it out with scissors and use the craft knife to cut between the toes if you need to.

Step 2. Place the foot on the blue foam and carefully draw around the edges with marker pen.

Step 3. Now, cut out the foam foot shape with scissors.

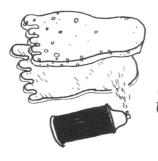
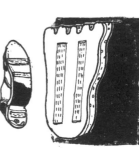

Step 4. Glue the foam foot and grey-board foot together with spray adhesive and leave to dry. Make the right foot in the same way. By creating the feet separately you'll avoid accidently making two left or right feet.

Step 5. Cut two lengths of Velcro and attach the hook sides to the board side of each foot. Cut the corresponding loop strips into small pieces and stick them onto the soles of a pair of shoes, then press the Velcroed shoes and foam feet firmly together. Now ink up the feet by either stamping them onto an inked slab or ink them up with a roller.

Step 6. To print a magnificent set of Bigfoot footprints, put on your shoes and walk across your paper (or floor, pavement, etc.).

Tip: Instead of using relief printing ink, try creating a poster-paint reservoir. Line a cat-litter tray with some more blue foam, pour plenty of paint in and allow the foam to soak it up. Place the Bigfoot feet into the tray to soak up the paint.

Rant Mullins, 1982

Vegetable printing

You will need:

Potatoes

Kitchen knife

Paper towel

Sharp pencil

Scalpel and lino-cutting tools

Water-based relief-printing ink, washable oil-based printing ink or oil-based ink pad

Ink roller and block

Paper

Most of us were introduced to print making with potato prints as children. It's an activity worth reaquainting yourself with – not only does it underscore the principles of relief printing, but the simplicity of the exercise also encourages a liberated, spontaneous approach. The starchy potato juices mix with any ink to give a watery, ethereal effect, too.

Step 1. You may want to slice your potatoes into square and rectangular blocks in preparation for carving, or you may prefer to incorporate the potato's organic shape as part of your image.

Step 2. Draw/incise lines into the surface with a pencil, or cut V-shaped gouges with the scalpel and lino-cutting tools.

Step 3. To remove large areas, use a kitchen knife – cut a 45-degree sloping rampart, followed by a horizontal cut.

Step 4. Blot the potato with a paper towel to absorb excess liquid.

Step 5. Ink the potato stamp with the roller. The potato will absorb the first few rolls of ink; wait until the ink is tacky before printing. Alternatively, stamp the potato onto some rolled-out ink or an oil-based ink pad.

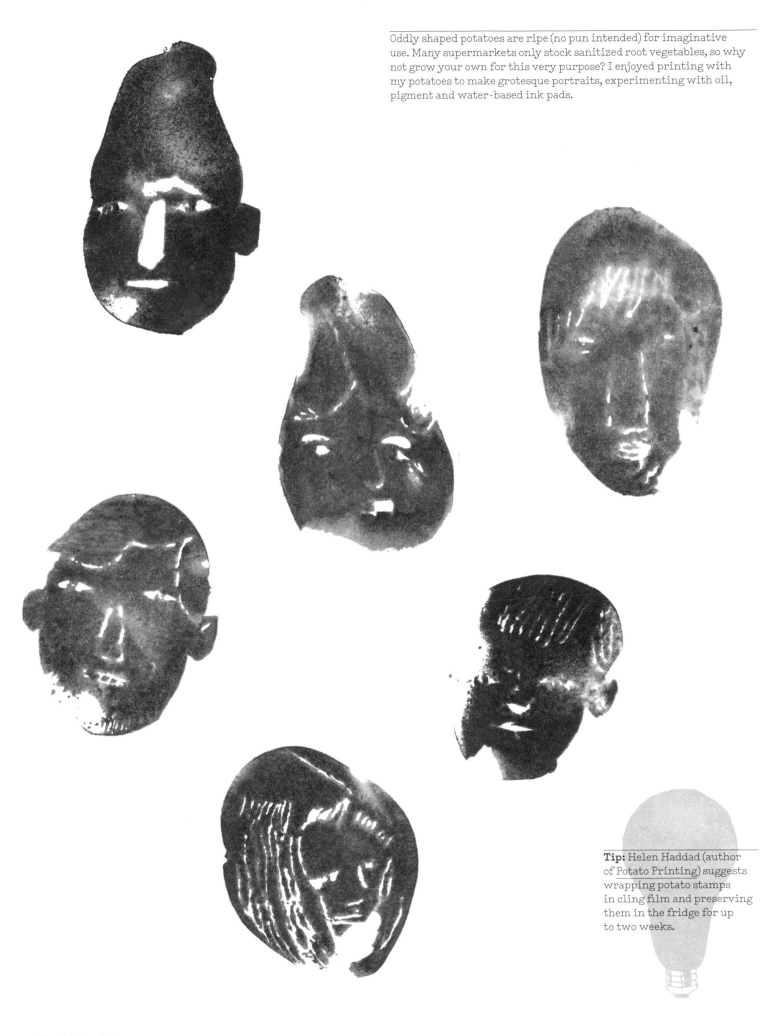

Oddly shaped potatoes are ripe (no pun intended) for imaginative use. Many supermarkets only stock sanitized root vegetables, so why not grow your own for this very purpose? I enjoyed printing with my potatoes to make grotesque portraits, experimenting with oil, pigment and water-based ink pads.

Tip: Helen Haddad (author of Potato Printing) suggests wrapping potato stamps in cling film and preserving them in the fridge for up to two weeks.

Large radishes, turnips, celeriac and yams also make for interesting prints. My yam prints were inspired by dried catfish spotted in the same market; my fish were then transformed into coelacanths due to the happy accident of the string-like, fossilized flesh of the vegetable.

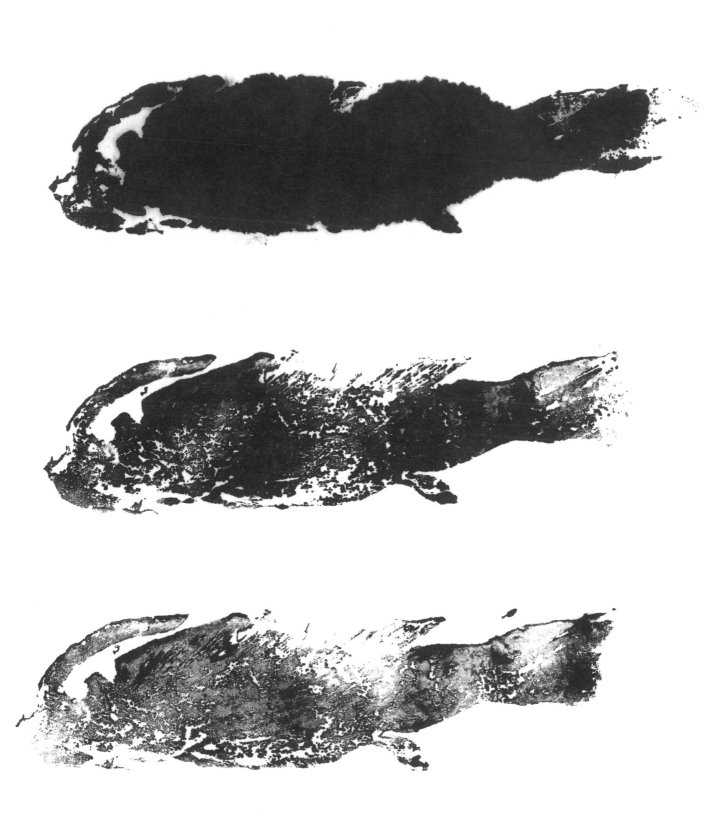

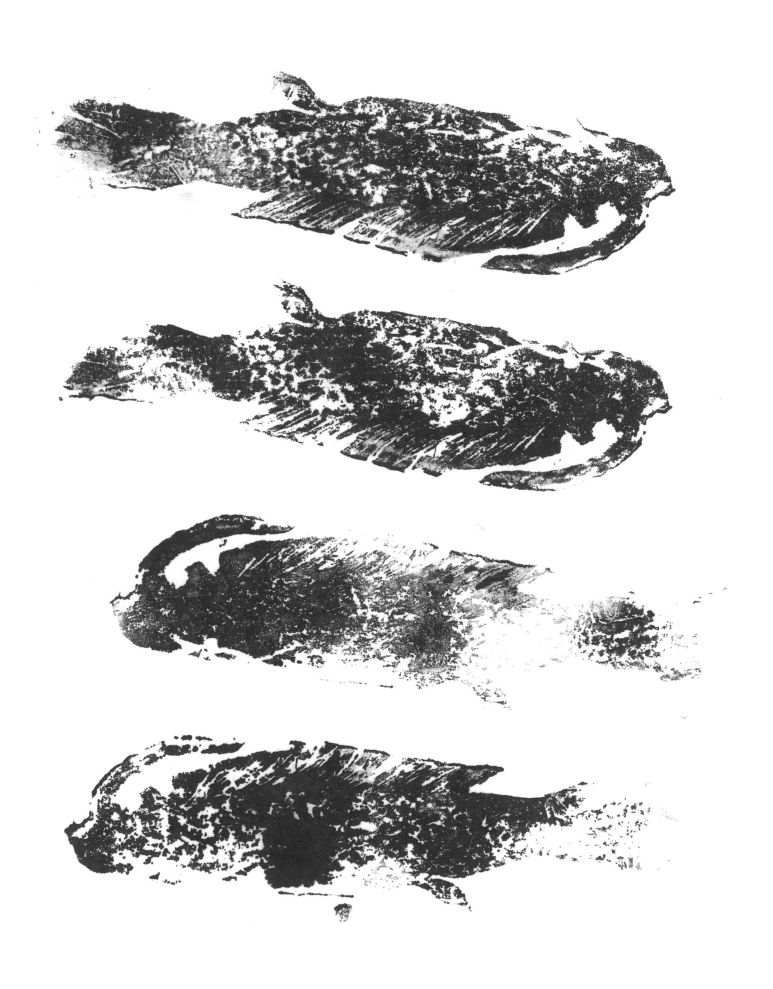

Creative rubbings

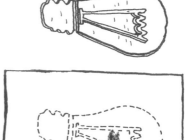

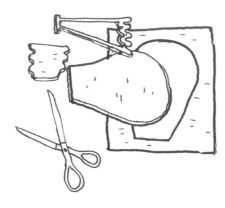

You will need:

Range of papers and card

Scalpel or scissors

Glue stick

Lightweight paper (try Redeem natural white 130 gsm, layout pad paper or newsprint; I like to use long A0 sheets of photocopy paper, scrounged from printing shops)

Brass-rubbing sticks (these will give the best results; graphite sticks are a good alternative)

In their simplest form, creative rubbings are taken from hand-constructed surfaces of assorted paper and card. In their richest guise, they are an amalgamation of several processes – frottage, collage and paper cutting.

Frottage is the technique of taking rubbings to create an impression of a surface. Collage consists of an intuitively assembled surface, built up from a varied selection of materials. Brown wrapping paper, paper mesh, tissue, corrugated cardboard, crepe paper and tracing paper all offer exciting possibilities. Enhance their qualities with carefully cut shapes, or jagged, torn edges; fold and score for straight lines, or scratch or cut paper to create hair-like lines.

Brass-rubbing sticks give an almost X-ray quality and will make distinctive impressions of all these layers, sometimes picking up both top and bottom layers, and even the work surface beneath them.

Step 1. Construct your chosen design using a range of card and paper; it can be abstract or figurative. Cut or tear, as required, and use a glue stick to fix things in place.

Step 2. Place a thin sheet of paper over the collage. Hold the brass-rubbing stick on its side and gradually rub it over the entire surface of the collage until a complete impression is revealed.

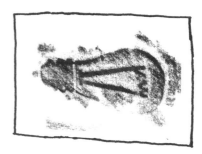

Step 3. The finished rubbing.

The joy of this process is that the collage surface can always be altered until a happy solution is reached. Consider tonal relationships for a richer, more satisfying result: rub harder for a darker tone and apply lighter pressure for understated greys.

These tonal relationships can also be enlivened with a marriage of lino-cut flat jet-black impressions, and the dual tones of photocopies – my Horse Hospital cinema poster 'Films of the Wood' (below), and LP insert created for the Eidetic Band (opposite page), were both constructed in this way. Form can also be described by determining the direction and weight of the rubbing stick's strokes.

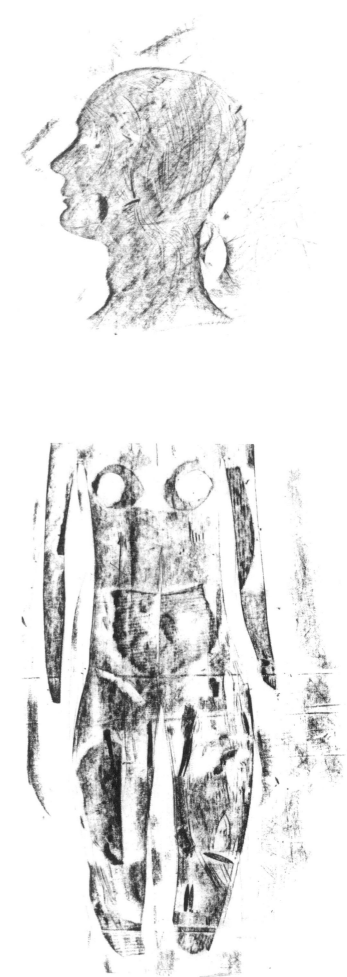

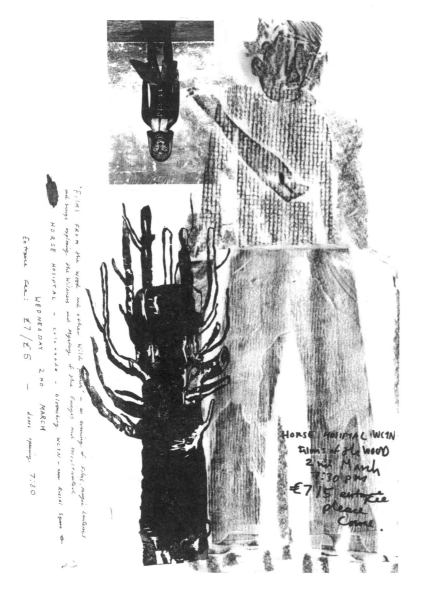

Plaster printing

You will need:

Water (approx. 2 litres/4 pints)
Cat-litter tray
Face mask (to prevent plaster inhalation)
Plaster of Paris (approx. 2.5 kg/5 lbs)
Rubber gloves
Oven and cooling rack
Small hacksaw
Tapestry needle or drypoint
etching tool
French or button polish
Old brush
Water-based relief-printing ink
or washable oil-based printing ink
Soft ink roller and block
Foam sheets
Soft paper and/or Japanese paper

I first encountered plaster printing in the work produced by Nigel Henderson and Eduardo Paolozzi for their joint applied-art enterprise, 'Hammer Prints', captured in a book of the same name. 'Sgraffito', one of their first wallpaper designs, took its name from the technique of scratching into layers of plaster to produce a design; it was based on photos of an inked impression of an engraved plaster block, and expressed the artists' fascination with children's scrawled wall drawings, Surrealist 'automatic' mark-making and Abstract Expressionism.

Step 1. Pour the water into the litter tray.

Step 2. In the open air and wearing a face mask, sprinkle the plaster into the water (not the other way round). Keep sprinkling until the plaster and water are almost equal, resembling a paddy field. Knock the sides of the tray to release any air bubbles.

Step 3. Wearing rubber gloves, break up any lumps of plaster in the mixture, then leave it to set.

Step 4. Remove the plaster from the tray by gently pulling back the tray walls.

Step 5. Transfer the plaster to a cooling rack and leave it in the sun for a few days to dry out completely. Alternatively, use an oven to speed up the process. Set the oven to its lowest temperature, place the plaster on an oven rack, allowing the warm air to circulate around it, and leave it for around 20 minutes, before gradually increasing the temperature to 70°C (150°F). Leave for a few hours.

Step 6. With the hacksaw, divide the plaster block into a number of smaller pieces.

Step 7. Carve your design into the smooth tray-bottom side of the block with the needle or etching tool. When completed, brush away any lingering plaster dust.

Step 8. Before you varnish the block, make sure the plaster is bone dry. The first varnish coat will quickly soak into the plaster; paint a further two or three thin coats, allowing the polish to dry in between each application. Leave on some scrap paper to dry completely.

Step 9. Gently stamp the block onto the rolled-out ink (an oil-based ink pad will also suffice). Place a piece of foam under your paper, to cushion the block and give a better print impression, then stamp your block onto the paper, pushing into the paper and foam.

Plaster prints have a primitive, ancient, grainy quality, and subjects seem fossilized and held in the past.

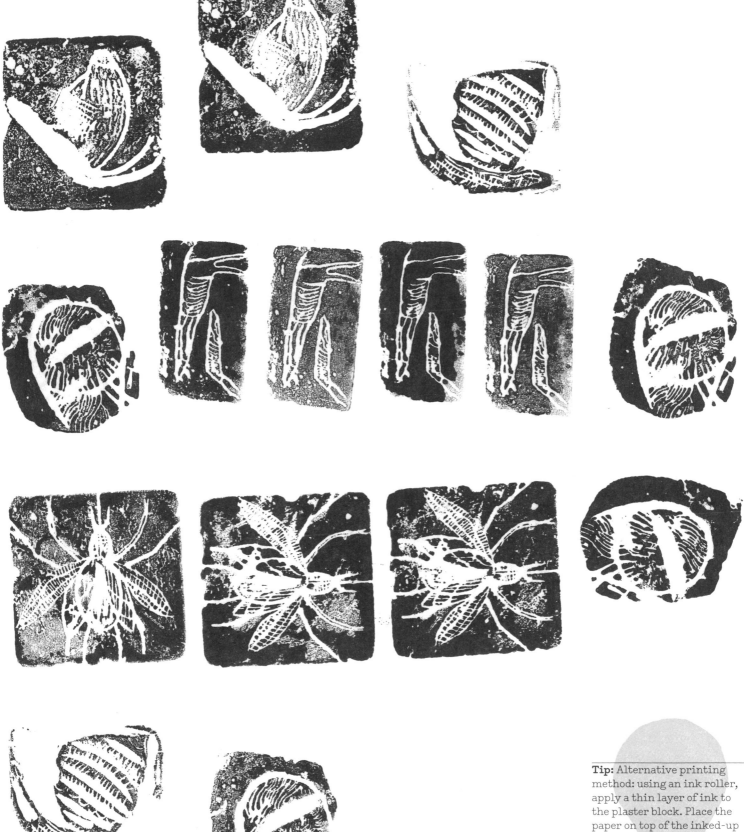

Tip: Alternative printing method: using an ink roller, apply a thin layer of ink to the plaster block. Place the paper on top of the inked-up block and, using a wooden spoon, apply firm pressure to the paper and block below. Peel off the print and leave to dry.

Printing with found objects

You will need:

A collection of bits and bobs
Varnish
Strong PVA adhesive
2 small brushes
Craft foam sheets
Scissors or scalpel
Small pieces of wood, handles or wooden game counters to act as grips
Ink pads and washable oil-based printing ink
Ink roller and block
Paper and newspaper

Travelling between home, work and studio, I always keep one eye out for interesting bits and pieces on the ground: haircombs, shoe soles, paper clips, washers, leaves, bottle tops, disposable forks, feathers, hooks, caps and bolts. Unidentifiable plastic, wood and metal pieces, snapped or fallen from their original source, hold a particular fascination.

By making direct prints (stamping or rolling ink onto an object's surface and printing directly from it), all found objects are simplified to abstract shape and texture. Through repetition this is heightened further – see Corinne Welch's prints of discarded string and foil pie tins (see page 150).

Look for potential stamp material wherever you go; search for flotsam and jetsam around buildings, the shoreline, under trees. Better still, take a friend and compare your collections on the journey home. We all discriminate according to personal preferences; objects I've disregarded always seem to create the best prints for my friends.

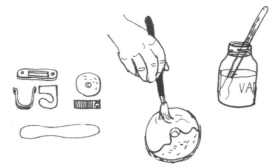

Step 1. Varnish any porous articles and leave them to dry on newspaper.

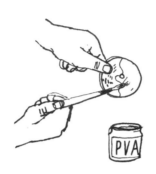

Step 2. Glue all your items onto a sheet of craft foam and leave to dry.

Step 3. Cut around each item with scissors or scalpel.

Step 4. Glue each article onto either a piece of scrap wood, a handle or a game counter.

Step 5. Experiment with an array of coloured ink pads (I prefer the oil-based variety) and thinly rolled washable oil-based printing inks.

Step 6. Placing some more cushioning foam sheet under the paper before printing will help create the perfect print.

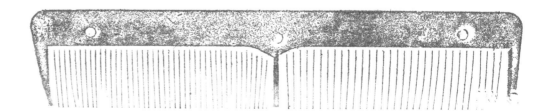

Each print will be different, depending on the amount of ink used, the pressure applied and the softness of the paper. Experiment with these variables until you're satisfied. You can also try combining print processes from previous chapters. Look after your stamp collection, too – they are beautiful objects in their own right.

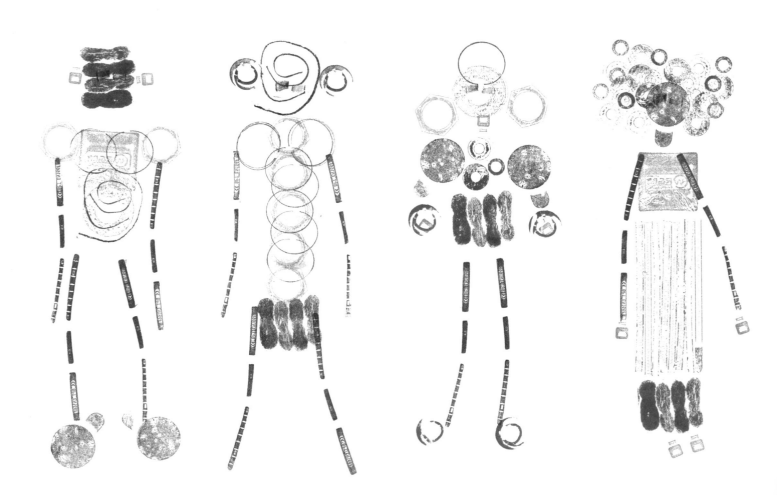

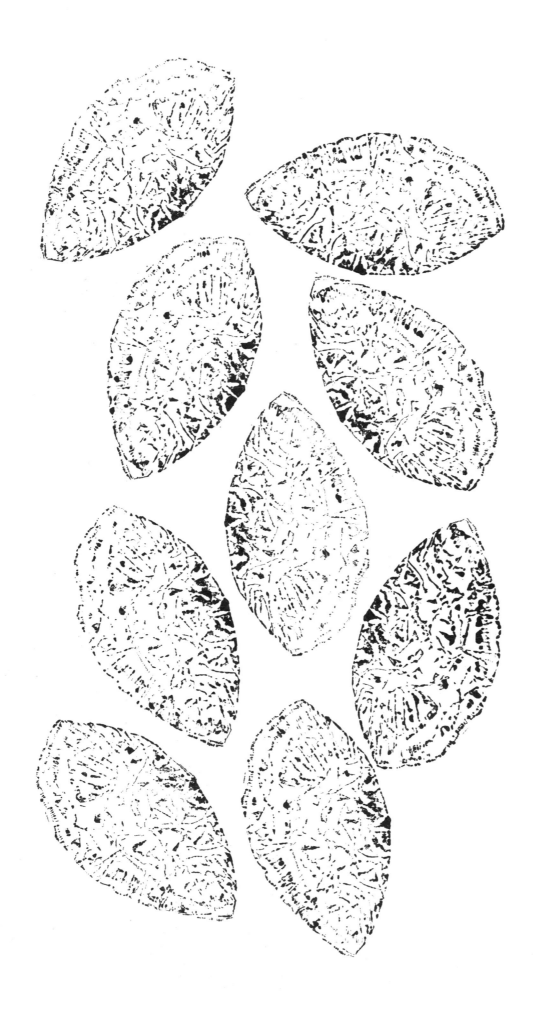

Printing with clay

You will need:

Clay
Talcum powder
Water-based relief-printing ink
Ink roller and block
Rolling pin
Paper
A collection of found objects: empty your pockets, look around your home, buy some plastic toys or go on a beachcombing expedition.

People of all ages and experience levels will find printing with clay a real pleasure. There is no need for specialist carving tools and designs are quick to make. The clay is either pushed onto a textured surface or objects are pressed onto rolled-out clay. Another advantage is clay's absorbency. During inking up and printing, a little of the clay will naturally mix with the ink, which speeds up the drying process considerably. I have known inks to dry in minutes that have previously taken hours.

Step 1. Make a ball of clay, no bigger than a tennis ball and press it firmly onto a work surface.

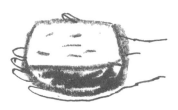

Step 2. You now have a perfectly flat-sided piece of clay, resembling half a potato.

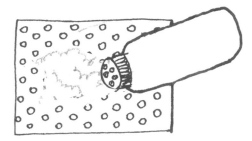

Step 3. Sprinkle a little talcum powder over your object. This will stop the clay from adhering to it.

Step 4. Press the flatside of the clay onto the object to create a clay relief.

Step 5. Roll out a little ink on the ink block.

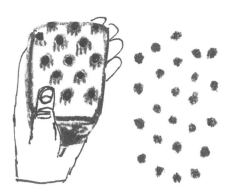

Step 6. Gently press the clay block into the ink, or gently roll a layer of ink over the clay relief. Then firmly stamp your paper.

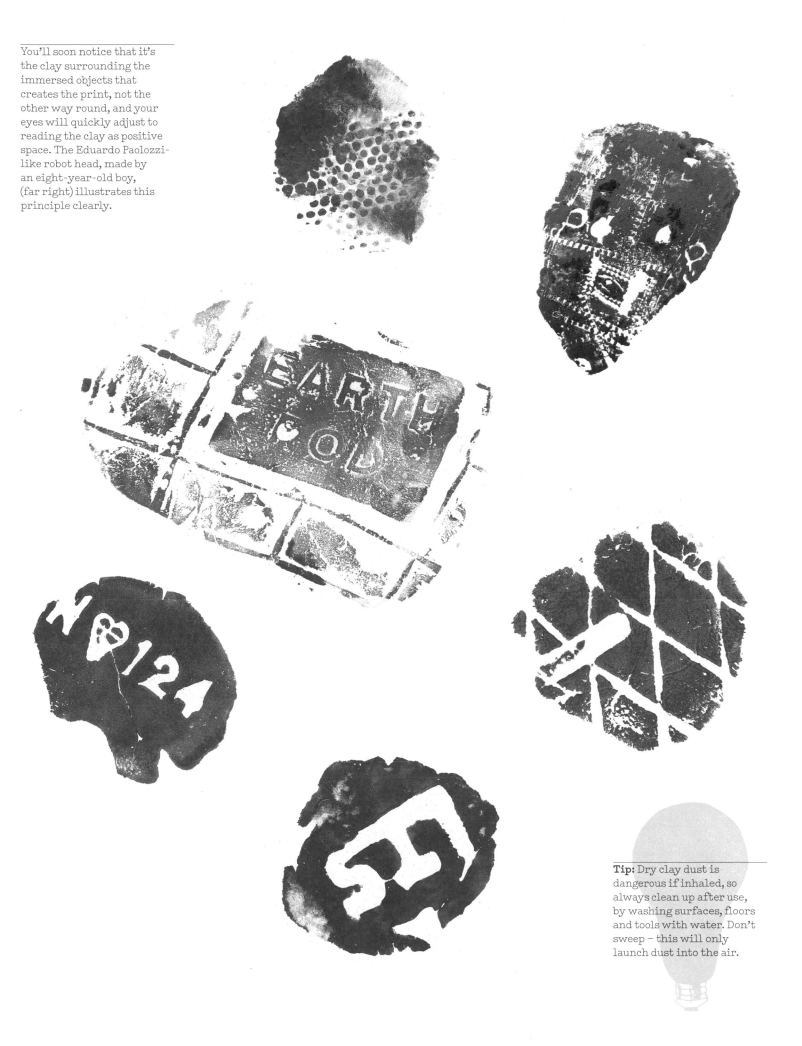

You'll soon notice that it's the clay surrounding the immersed objects that creates the print, not the other way round, and your eyes will quickly adjust to reading the clay as positive space. The Eduardo Paolozzi-like robot head, made by an eight-year-old boy, (far right) illustrates this principle clearly.

Tip: Dry clay dust is dangerous if inhaled, so always clean up after use, by washing surfaces, floors and tools with water. Don't sweep – this will only launch dust into the air.

Plasticine

Plasticine is a good alternative to clay – it holds ink well, and has the added bonus of not sticking to things. The downside is that after one or two prints it loses its shape, although this can create interestingly fluid effects. Corinne Welch's work demonstrates this well – her electric hob-shaped prints (below) have a lively fried egg/lollipop quality to them, while her prints of carpenter's plastic shims take on the look of melting targets or train tunnels (facing page).

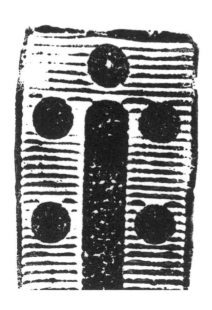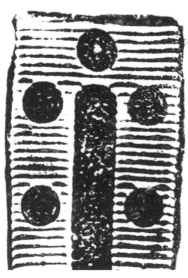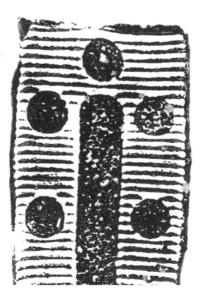

Further reading

Rubber Stamping

George L. Thomson, Rubber Stamps & How to Make Them, New York, Pantheon Books, 1982.

John Held Jr, Rubber Stamp Art, Bertiolo, Italy, AAA Edizioni, 1999.

Sandra Mizumoto Posey, Rubber Soul: Rubber Stamps & Correspondence Art, Jackson, University Press of Mississippi, 1996.

John K.Miller & Lowry Thompson, The Rubber Stamp Album, the complete guide to making everything prettier, weirder and funnier. How and where to buy over 5,000 rubber stamps. And how to use them. New York, Workman Publishing, 1978.

Oshima Natsuko, Tokyoite Stamp, Tokyo, 2015.

Vincent Sardon, Le Tampographe Sardon, Paris, L'Association, 2012.

Printmaking

Caspar Williamson, Low-Tech Print: Contemporary Hand-Made Printing, London, Laurence King Publishing, 2013.

Beth Grabowski, Printmaking: A Complete Guide to Materials and Processes, London, Laurence King Publishing, 2009.

Christine Schmidt, Print Workshop, New York, Potter Craft, 2011.

Robin Capon, Introducing Abstract Printmaking, London, BT Batsford, 1973.

Peter Green, Introducing Surface Printing, London, BT Batsford, 1967.

Robin Tanner, Children's Work in Block Printing, Leicester, Reeves Dryard Press, 1958.

Susanne Strose, Potato Printing, (Little Craft Book series), New York, Sterling Publishing, 1969.

Helen R. Haddad, Potato Printing, New York, Crowell,1981.

Chris Treweek and Jonathan Zietlyn with the Islington Bus Co, The Alternative Printing Handbook, Middlesex, Penguin Books, 1983.

Heather Amery & Anne Civardi, The Knowhow Book of Print and Paint, London, Usborne Publishing, 1975.

Henry Pluckrose, A Craft Collection, London, Evans Brothers Ltd, 1973.

Laye Andrew, Creative Rubbings, London, BT Batsford, 1967.

Mail Art & Artistamps

John Held Jr, Small Scale Subversion: Mail Art & Artistamps, North Carolina, lulu.com, 2015.

John Held Jr, Mail Art: An Annotated Bibliography, Lanham, Scarecrow Press, 1991.

John Tingey, The Englishman who Posted Himself and Other Curious Objects New York, Princeton Architectural Press, 2010.

Harriet Russell, Envelopes: A Puzzling Journey Through the Royal Mail, London, Allison and Busby, 2008.

Bookbinding

Esther K.Smith, How to Make Books: Fold, Cut & Stitch Your Way to a One-of-a-Kind Book. New York, Potter Craft, 2007.

Alisa Golden, Making Handmade Books: 100+ Bindings, Structures & Forms, New York, Lark Books, 2011.

Sarah Bodman, Creating Artists' Books (Printmaking Handbooks), New York, Watson-Guptill, 2005.

Last but not least …

Joan Rendell, Collecting out of doors, London, Routledge & Kegan Paul, 1976.

Corita Kent & Jan Steward, Learning by Heart Teaching to Free the Creative Spirit, New York, Allworth Press, 2008.

On the Web

Rubber Stamp Madness: www.rsmadness.com

TAM Rubber Stamp Archive: tamrubberstamparchive.blogspot.co.uk

Vincent Sardon website: le-tampographe-sardon.blogspot.co.uk

International Union of Mail Artists: iuoma-network.ning.com

Mail Artist Index: mailartists.wordpress.com

Films & Animation

Thomas Hicks – Night Watchman's Blues: thomashicks.co.uk/Nightwatchman-s-Blues

Emma Ehrling, Cockroach Sketchcycle: vimeo.com/126698078

John Held Jr: KQED Spark Film of John Held Jr Mail collection www.youtube.com/watch?v=BZsjJExwF_0

Roller Printing Film: www.youtube.com/watch?v=eF5FDW3b9bM

Specialist suppliers

Rubber Stamping

Blade Rubber Stamps Ltd 12 Bury Place, London WC1A 2JL. www.bladerubber.co.uk

Printmaking

Intaglio Printmaker Playhouse Court, 62 Southwark Bridge Road, Southwark, London SE1 0AS. www.intaglioprintmaker.com

Bookbinding and paper

Shepherd Falkiners 30 Gillingham Street, London SW1V 1HU. store.bookbinding.co.uk

J. Hewit & Sons Ltd 12 Nettlehill Road, Houstoun Industrial Estate, Livingston, West Lothian, EH54 5DL. www.hewit.com

John Purcell Paper 15 Rumsey Road, London SW9 0TR. www.johnpurcell.net

Arboreta Papers 8 Willway Street, Bristol, BS3 4BG. www.arboretapapers.co.uk

Miscellaneous

Scafclad www.scafclad.co.uk (Scaffolding protection foam suppliers)

White Winds Ltd www.whitewinds.co.uk (brass rubbing sticks)

Alec Tiranti Ltd Clay and Plaster of Paris Suppliers 27 Warren Street, London, W1T 5NB & 3 Pipers Court, Berkshire Drive, Thatcham, Berkshire, RG19 4ER. www.tiranti.co.uk

Home Base www.homebase.co.uk ('Mangers' 22mm foam pipe lagging)

Leyland SDM www.leylandsdm.co.uk (small radiator rollers and tiny 1/16 inch brass tubing)

Preservation Equipment Ltd www.preservationequipment.com (gummed paper for faux stamps)

A.P Kirby Swanfield Street, London, E2 7DS (foam supplier for the Bigfoot printing project)

Index

Index

Picture credits

All artwork by Stephen Fowler, all photography by Ida Riveros except where credited. All efforts have been made to credit the prints in this book, in the few cases where I was unable to, I have stated where and when they were printed.

7   Fairytale character multiple stamp, Rob Ryan, 2012.
8   The Wonderful World of Fleming-Joffe cover drawing, Andy Warhol and Julia Warhola, 1961. The Andy Warhol Museum, Pittsburgh; Founding Collection, Contribution The Andy Warhol Foundation for the Visual Arts, Inc. 1998.1.1184.
9   Immaculate Heart College Art Department Rules, David Mekelberg, c. 1968. Reprinted with permission of the Corita Art Center, Immaculate Heart Community, Los Angeles.
10   Tokyoite Stamp figures, Natsuko Oshima 2015.
11   We sit starving amidst our gold, Jeremy Deller, British Pavilion, Venice Biennale, 2013.
23   'Bearded gentleman', Tavan Maneetapho, 2011; 'Dinosaur head', Abagail Mortimer, 2015.
30   'Black claws', Elisha Marshall, 2004; 'Mermaid', Lorna Scobie, 2010; 'Skeleton/Coffin', Tim King, 2010; 'Bird & cat' by a 1st-year Kingston Illustration degree student during a workshop in 2013; 'Monsters' Matt Ferguson & friends, 2006.
31   'Firey Monsieur', Helen Davies, 2007; 'Three Eyes King', 'Flask & cup', 'Drummer', 'Skull', 'Ouch', 'Quavers', 'Hand', John Bently, 1983–2014; 'Prague coffee cup' and 'Beer glass', Zeel, 1991; 'Pig' and 'Cow', Hannah McNally, 2015.
34   'Bowler hatted business men', by a participant at a workshop at the Bristol Artist Book Event (BABE) at the Arnolfini, 2011.
35   Reportage rubber stamp drawing, Yan Dan Wong, 2015.
36   'Toe to toe little people', Lily Xue, 2015.
37   'Architectural arches', Jackie Kirk, 2015; 'Cacti', Ruby Smith, 2014; 'Tree branch', Rosie Bell Ryott, 2014.
43   Repeat patterns, Jantze Tullett, 2015.
44   'Button maze' book, Haley Dixon, 2004; 'Pop-up ant farm', Alexandra Czinczel, 2012.
46   Exquisite corpses, Bjørn Rune Stainer-Lie, 2010.

47   'Bear/fish & dog/caterpillar' exquisite corpses, Philippe Nash, Izzy Sempill, Willow Twinam Cauchi, 2015; 'Fish-headed/King-headed/Queen-headed' exquisite corpses, Katie Delaney, Hazel Grainger, Charlotte Hall, Vicky Harrison, Arcangela Regis, Sarah Bodman, Stephen Fowler, 2011.
48–9   Identikit portraits by a small group of 2nd-year Kingston Illustration degree students during a workshop, photographed by Stephen Fowler, 2008.
50–1   Rubber stamp portraits, Rose Blake, Mark El-khatib, Dan Frost, Paddy Molloy, Alice Moloney & Mike Redmond, 2010.
53   'I moustache you a question', Amanda Revell, 2012; 'Eraserheads' and 'Stampede' rubber stamp artist book covers, Katie Delaney, Hazel Grainger, Charlotte Hall, Vicky Harrison, Arcangela Regis, Sarah Bodman, photographed by Stephen Fowler, 2011.
54   Liver & Lights, No 23, 100 Books inside cover, John Bently. Published by Liver & Lights Scriptorium, 1996; 'Demoniac Evangelist' font, Zeel 2015.
55   'Shadow' font, Edwood Burn, 2011.
56   Gravenhurst's 'Nightwatchman's Blues' record sleeve, Thomas Hicks. Released by Warp records, 2008.
57   'Cops and Robbers', Nammi Eu, 2015; 'Dollar sign', Katie Hammett, 2014.
68   'Flowers', 'Leeks' and 'Turnips', Paula Lovatt, 2010.
69   'Rainbow toadstools' by a workshop participant at Shepherd/Falkiners Fine Paper, 2011.
82–3   Model: Sasha Ilyukevich, photographed by Stephen Fowler, 2015.
84   'Deep sea diver in jar', 'Head with glasses', photographed by Stephen Fowler, 2015. 'Skeleton' and 'deep sea diver and graffiti jelly fish', photographed by Steve Tarry, 2015.
85   'Landmarks Wayfinding' and 'Mark Making Trail' event, photograph courtesy of Edinburgh Printmakers. Rubber stamps designed, printed and photographed by David Lemm, 2015.
90   'Dinosaur', 'beetle', 'egg' and 'rose', Jo Cook (aka Bucky Fleur), Eve Rei Archer and Stephen Fowler, 2015; Postcard (bottom), Jo Cook (aka Bucky Fleur), 2015.
91   Mail art (top), Jo Cook (aka Bucky Fleur) 2015; Mail art (bottom), Jo Cook (aka Bucky Fleur) and Stephen Fowler, 2015.
92   'Rabbit' mail art, John Bently and (Nervous) Stephen Fowler, 2015.
93   Mail art, Desdemona Mccannon, 2015.

98–9   Stickers (far right), Zeel, 2009; 'Milk' matchbox, Helen Allsebrook, 2010.
100–1   'Travailleurs de tous les pays, uniseeez-vous!' and 'J'en ai rien à foutre' stamps, Vincent Sardon, 2014.
102–3   Large packing foam stamps and 'flower', Zeel, 2013.
104–5   'Shield' patch, 'Pigwool' foam stamp, 'Gore Boars' stamp and 'Pigwool' giant fabric patch, Zeel, 2015.
109   Rubber stamped iced biscuits photographed by Stephen Smart, 2015.
116–7   Angular lined printed background (behind horse riders), Lily Arnold, 2013.
118–9   Diamond carved roller (bottom left), Amy Harris, 2013; Angular lined carved roller (next to bird roller), Lily Arnold, 2013.
122   'Cars at night' roller repeat, Danny Stanton, 2013.
124   Multilayered roller repeat, Chloe Alexander, 2014.
137   Rant Mullins with a set of fake Bigfoot feet, 1982. PA Images.
150   'String', Corinne Welch, 2014; Found object printed figures, Cathy Brett, 2015.
151   'Foil tin pie', Corinne Welch, 2014.
153   'Robot head' created during a workshop at 'We're Here Now' Banbury & Bicester College, photographed by Neil Mabbs.
154–5   Plasticine prints, Corinne Welch, 2014.

Acknowledgements

I would like to thank all the contributing artists, illustrators and rubber stampers – including John Bently, Jo Cook, Alexandra Czinczel, Jeremy Deller, Thomas Hicks, David Lemm, Paddy Molloy, Natsuko Oshima, Vincent Sardon, Jantze Tullett, Corinne Welch and Zeel – for their generosity and keen involvement.

Thanks to Rob Ryan (the scribe), Sasha Ilyukevich for bearing his chest, Rono Takagawa and Felicity Greenland (the translators), and Amaia and David Brown (the encouragers).

Many thanks to Sarah Bodman, Martin Carrolchick, Sarah Britten-Jones, and Gina Mumford for their expert advice and encouragement. I would especially like to say thank you to Rachael Matthews for all her time and invaluable help.

A big thank you to the team at Laurence King Publishing: to Sophie Drysdale for initiating the project – it has been an exciting and an all-consuming experience! – as well as Melissa Danny, Ida Riveros, Davina Cheung and the brilliant Sophie Wise for her patience, humour and guidance, enabling the project to develop in its own particular fashion. And of course another big thank to John Dowling for his book-design magic.

I would also like to express my gratitude to Shepherds Falkiners, London, and the following institutions and courses for allowing artwork by their brilliant students to be reproduced: Kingston University's Illustration and Animation BA (Hons) degree, Banbury and Bicester College's Creative Arts and Design Practice foundation degree, University of the West of England's Centre for Fine Print Research, the University of the Creative Arts' Illustration MA degree, Lincoln University's Graphics BA (Hons) degree.

Thanks too to Mole and his adapted-roller inspiration, and to Eileen Collings and Steve Hoskins for introducing me to alternative printmaking library books and rubber stamping.

Thanks to Barrie Tullett – you know why! And to Rocky – thanks for being such a patient neighbour.

And, finally, thank you to Helen and William, to whom this book is dedicated.